GCSE RELIGIOUS STUDIES
THE REVELATION OF GOD
AND THE CHRISTIAN CHURCH

COLOURPOINT
EDUCATIONAL

Rewarding Learning

Juliana Gilbride

Anne Hughes

© Juliana Gilbride and Colourpoint Books 2009

ISBN: 978 1 906578 33 6

First Edition
First Impression

Layout and design: Colourpoint Books
Printed by: W&G Baird Ltd, Antrim

COLOURPOINT EDUCATIONAL

Colourpoint Books
Colourpoint House
Jubilee Business Park
21 Jubilee Road
Newtownards
County Down
Northern Ireland
BT23 4YH

Tel: 028 9182 6339
Fax: 028 9182 1900
E-mail: info@colourpoint.co.uk
Web site: www.colourpoint.co.uk

The Authors

Juliana Gilbride, B.Ed (Hons), M.Ed, was part of a team of teachers who revised the Religious Studies GCSE Specification for CCEA (for first teaching in 2009). She is a Revisor for GCSE Religious Studies for CCEA, and has fifteen years experience of teaching Religious Studies in Northern Ireland.

Anne Hughes B.Ed (Hons) has 18 years experience teaching Religious Education in post primary school both at GCSE and 'A' Level. She is Assistant Head of the Religious Education Department at Our Lady and St Patrick's College, Belfast and has 16 years examining experience at CCEA.

Author's acknowledgements

Thanks to Rev Steve Stockman, Canon Walter Lewis, Rev Ken Newell and Rachel Gardiner. Thanks to all the churches that gave kind permission for photographs to be used. Special thanks to Martin, Tom and Kate.
-Juliana Gilbride

Thanks to Sheila Johnston at Colourpoint and Donna Finlay at CCEA for the opportunity to work on the book, and to Michael Spence at Colourpoint. Particular thanks to the SVP Conference at Our Lady and Saint Patrick's College, Belfast; to Dominic Kealey and Angela Killen; Claire and Stephen McCaffrey; and to Maeve Byrne, Rachel McCloskey and Hannah McGrath for their wonderful insight into the Community Service work carried out by the students of Our Lady and Saint Patrick's College, Belfast. A special thank you to Gerry, Rónán, Éile and Tiarnán for their support and patience.
-Anne Hughes

The acknowledgements on page 128 constitute an extension of this copyright page.

CONTENTS

CHAPTER 1 BACKGROUND TO THE GOSPELS   5

Geographical Context 5
Historical and Political Context 7
Religious and Social Background 8

CHAPTER 2 THE IDENTITY OF JESUS   12

Titles of Jesus 12
Key Events Surrounding The Birth of Jesus 13
Jesus' Baptism and Temptations 16
Peter's Declaration of Faith 20
The Transfiguration 20

CHAPTER 3 THE TEACHING OF JESUS   22

The Implications of Discipleship 22
Jesus' Teaching on Prayer 24
Jesus' Teaching on Forgiveness 26
Jesus' Teaching on Wealth and Poverty 28
The Parable of the Sower 29

CHAPTER 4 THE DEEDS OF JESUS   31

Jesus' Dealings with Religious Leaders 31
Jesus' Dealings with Women 33
Jesus' Dealings with a Social Outcast 35

CHAPTER 5 THE DEATH AND RESURRECTION OF JESUS   36

The Last Supper 36
Jesus' Arrest 38
Jesus' Trials 38
Jesus' Death 40
Jesus' Resurrection 43

CHAPTER 6 CHRISTIAN WORSHIP   46

The Development of the Christian Church 46
Styles of Worship 47
The Tradition of Singing and Music 48
Different Types of Prayer and their Purpose in Christian Worship 50
Orders of Service 55
The Importance of the Bible 63
The Importance of Preaching 64

CHAPTER 7 CHURCH ARCHITECTURE AND FURNITURE   66

Church Architecture 66
Church Furniture 68

CHAPTER 8 CHURCH FESTIVALS   75

Advent 76
Christmas 79
Epiphany 84
The Easter Cycle 84
Pentecost 92
Saint's Days 92
Harvest 93

CHAPTER 9 SACRAMENTS AND ORDINANCES   95

Baptism 95
Eucharist or Communion 107

CHAPTER 10 THE ROLE OF THE CHURCH IN CONTEMPORARY SOCIETY   115

The Contribution of the Christian Churches
to Peace and Reconciliation in a Divided Society 115

The Contribution of the Christian Church
to Local Community and Community Cohesion 117

The Challenge to the Christian Church of
Changing Moral, Social and Cultural Values 120

INDEX 126

For your folder   In a Group   Further Thinking

Chapter 1

BACKGROUND TO THE GOSPELS

The word 'Gospel' means 'good news'. It is comes from the Anglo-Saxon *god spel*, which can mean 'spell it out', 'speak out' or 'proclaim'. In the Bible the Gospels proclaim the good news about Jesus.

There are four Gospels with four different writers: Matthew, Mark, Luke and John. Each records the events of Jesus' life, death and resurrection. Three of the Gospels – Matthew, Mark and Luke – are very similar in content and structure. These are called the 'Synoptic Gospels'. The word *synoptic* means 'shared view'. Many passages from these three Gospels can be placed side by side to show how similar they are – for example, the story of Jesus' baptism and temptations (Matthew 3:13–4:11; Mark 1:9–13; Luke 3:21–22, 4:1–13). The fourth account of Jesus' life, John's Gospel, is very different in style and content to the other three.

Before we look at the important events in the life of Jesus it will be useful to find out as much as possible about the place and time in which he lived. Background information that helps us to understand those events includes the geographical, political, social and religious background of Palestine at the time of Jesus.

GEOGRAPHICAL CONTEXT

Jesus lived in a place called Palestine. Today this land is occupied by the countries of Israel and Palestine. It is an extremely important place for Jews, Christians and Muslims, for whom it has deep, sacred significance.

Palestine in the First Century

- Region ruled by Archelaus (later ruled by Roman governors)
- Region ruled by Herod Antipas
- Region ruled by Philip

PHOENICIA
Mt Hermon
Tyre
Caesarea Philippi
ITUREA
GALILEE
Ptolemais
Capernaum
Bethsaida
Lake Galilee
Tiberias
Nazareth
Cana
Nain
Gadara
Mediterranean Sea
Caesarea
DECAPOLIS
SAMARIA
Sebaste (Samaria)
Gerasa
Joppa
PEREA
Jericho
Jerusalem
Bethany
Bethlehem
Judean Desert
Dead Sea
JUDEA
Masada
IDUMEA
NABATAEA

The River Jordan

The Jordan River runs from the Uplands of Galilee into the Sea of Galilee, then through the Rift Valley and into the Dead Sea. It splits Palestine down the middle.

The Sea of Galilee

The northern area around **Galilee** is where Jesus spent much of his life. The Sea of Galilee is really a large lake 13 miles long and 7 miles across.

Galilee, Samaria and Judea

Find the **River Jordan** on the map. If you look to the left of it you will see three main regions – **Galilee** at the top, **Samaria** in the middle and **Judea** underneath. It is mainly within these regions that the ministry of Jesus took place, although he does travel beyond them. You may also recognise the place names of some of the towns, where important events happened in the life of Jesus, such as the town of Bethlehem and the city of Jerusalem.

As you work your way through this book and come across the names of different places it is a good idea to look back to this map to see exactly where the places were.

TIP

Bethlehem

Bethlehem is a town in Judea where Jesus was born. It was prophesied that the Messiah would be born in the 'town of David': Bethlehem (Micah 5:2).

The Wilderness of Judea

To the east of the Uplands of Judea lies the Wilderness of Judea, a desolate area where John the Baptist lived and where Jesus was tempted.

Jerusalem

A scale model of Jerusalem at the time of Jesus.

Jerusalem was the capital city of Palestine. At the time of Jesus it had many visitors and the streets were full of traders and travellers, many of whom were Jews who went to visit Jerusalem to carry out their religious duties at festival times.

HISTORICAL AND POLITICAL CONTEXT

Palestine was a popular target for invading nations. Its central geographical position made it an important trade route and useful military base. As a result it had been governed by a number of different rulers and influenced by different cultures

In 63 BC Palestine came to be under the control of the Romans after General Pompey captured Jerusalem. At the time of Jesus' birth, around 4 BC, the Emperor of the Roman Empire was **Caesar Augustus**. Palestine was governed by **Herod the Great** (37–4 BC).

When Herod died in 4 BC the Jews wanted the Emperor Augustus to end the Herodian rule of Palestine but the Emperor refused and the kingdom was divided between three of Herod's sons:

- Herod Antipas, who took charge of **Galilee** and Perea;
- Herod Archelaus, who took charge of **Judea and Samaria**; and
- Philip the Tetrarch, who took charge of Iturea and Trachonitis. (The map on page 5 shows these territories.)

Out of the three, Archelaus was a brutal, corrupt and incompetent leader. In AD6 the Romans replaced him with a government official known as a procurator. The procurator answered directly to Rome and was responsible for collecting taxes,

keeping the peace and administering justice, which included the power to pass the death sentence. In AD26–36 the procurator was called Pontius Pilate.

The Roman Army

The Roman army was an extremely well organised force. It was highly disciplined, strong and feared throughout the Roman Empire. As Palestine was occupied by the Romans it was common to see Roman soldiers stationed throughout the country.

The majority of the Jewish people despised the presence of the Romans in Palestine and regarded them as bullies, and outsiders in their land. Some Jews (for example, the Zealots) showed their contempt for the Romans through violence and acts of aggression.

The Sanhedrin

The Sanhedrin was the highest Jewish Council in Palestine. There were 71 members made up of religious leaders called Pharisees and Sadducees. It had some power, although it was limited. For example, the Sanhedrin did not have the power to pass the death sentence. The chairman or leader of the Sanhedrin was the High Priest.

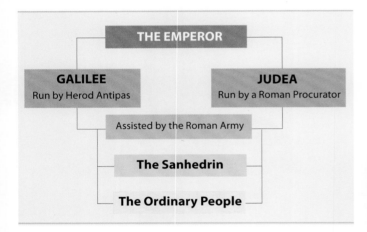

THE EMPEROR	
GALILEE Run by Herod Antipas	**JUDEA** Run by a Roman Procurator
Assisted by the Roman Army	
The Sanhedrin	
The Ordinary People	

Tax collectors

Palestine was taxed by the Romans. Local Jewish people worked as tax collectors, gathering money for the Roman government. These people were hated and considered 'sinners' because of what they did:

- They worked for the Roman government, the occupying force in Palestine and therefore were regarded as traitors

- They had a reputation for being dishonest. It was perfectly normal for tax collectors to charge people a larger amount than was required by the Romans, so they could take a large profit themselves.
- They were not able to give money to charity because it was regarded as 'unclean'.

RELIGIOUS AND SOCIAL BACKGROUND

The religion in Palestine at the time of Jesus was **Judaism**. Judaism is one of the oldest monotheistic religions in the world ('monotheism' is the belief that there is only one God).

The Jewish Law

The first five books of the Old Testament contain the Jewish Law or 'Torah', which was given by God to Moses on Mount Sinai. The Jews' ancestors had promised to keep the law in return for being God's chosen people. Over a thousand years later, at the time of Jesus, the law was still extremely important to the Jews.

The Jewish religious leaders who interpreted the law were called the **Scribes**. In the Gospels they were often called the 'teachers of the law'. People had great respect for them and would stand up in respect if a Scribe passed by. A lot of discussion took place between the Scribes over the meaning of the law. The interpretation of the law that they agreed upon was called the **Oral Law**. This was a list of complex rules and regulations meant to help people keep the Ten Commandments.

The Sabbath

The word 'sabbath' comes from the Hebrew word *shabat* which means 'to cease'. The Sabbath was a day of rest which began at sunset on Friday evening and lasted until sunset on Saturday evening. All work stopped on the Sabbath day.

Gentiles

A Gentile is anyone who is not Jewish. Many of them worshipped lots of different gods. Some Gentiles were known as 'God-fearers'. They may have followed some Jewish laws or beliefs, but they were not full Jews.

The Synagogue

A synagogue is a place of worship for Jews. The word 'synagogue' comes from a Greek word meaning 'gathering of people' or 'bringing together'. In Palestine at the time of Jesus there were synagogues in every town that had at least ten men. As well as being a house of prayer, a synagogue was a place of teaching where the scriptures were read and explained. Synagogue services were led and organised by elders.

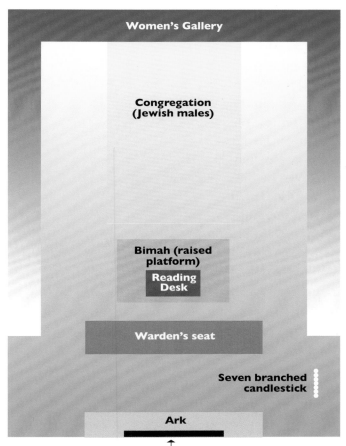

Women's Gallery

Congregation (Jewish males)

Bimah (raised platform)

Reading Desk

Warden's seat

Seven branched candlestick

Ark

Ten Commandments overhead

The ruins of the Kfar Bar'am synagogue in upper Galilee.

The Temple

At the time of Jesus, Herod the Great was building a new Temple on the site of the old. It was completely destroyed by the Romans in AD70. All that remains of it now is the western wall, known as the 'Wailing Wall'.

Jews praying at the 'Wailing Wall'

The Temple was important because it was the only place where the Jews could offer sacrifices to God. Sacrifices were made by a priest on the altar of sacrifice (see diagram).

The Temple was spacious and contained one outer court and four enclosed courts:

The Outer Court: The Court of Gentiles

This courtyard was inside the wall of the Temple and was the only part of the Temple grounds that a Gentile (non-Jew) was allowed to enter. Temple markets were held here which catered for worshippers' activities. Money-changers provided suitable coins for the Temple offering – coins with Caesar's head were not allowed. Animals for sacrifice were sold at the Temple markets as they had already been checked for purity by the Temple inspectors.

The Court of Women

Jewish women were allowed to enter this court but were not allowed to go beyond it. The Temple treasury for offerings of money was kept there.

The Court of Israel

This court encircled three sides of the Holy Place. Jewish men were allowed into this court. It was a place where men and priests came to pray.

The Holy Place

The Holy Place was where the Priests could go to burn incense. It was divided into two by a thick curtain called 'The Veil'. Once a year, on the Day of Atonement, the High Priest went beyond the Veil into the Holy of Holies. The Holy of Holies was thought of as the place where God was most present.

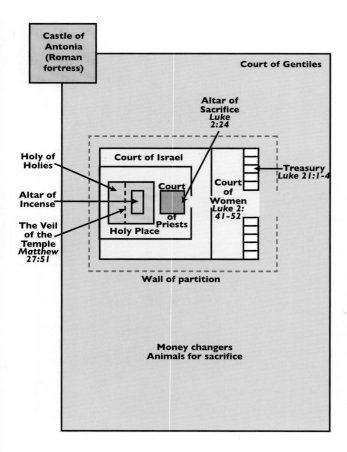

RELIGIOUS GROUPS WITHIN JUDAISM

The Pharisees

As you learn about the life and ministry of Jesus you will hear a lot about his relationship with the Pharisees and how they opposed Jesus on many occasions. They were the largest and most influential of the religious groups within Judaism in the first century. Jesus believed that many of them did not have genuine faith but were obsessed with keeping petty laws. He often called them hypocrites.

The word *Pharisee* means 'separated one'. They aimed to separate themselves from anything that they believed would make them 'unclean'. This included Romans, Gentiles, and any other Jews who had become 'unclean'.

The Pharisees had a strong belief that a Messiah, or saviour, would come from God to deliver the Jews from their hardships, leading them into a time of religious and political good fortune. They also believed in life after death and bodily resurrection.

The Sadducees

These were a small group of wealthy, upper class religious leaders who looked down upon the ordinary people. Most of them were priests. They tried to be friendly with the Romans to keep the power that they held. They differed from the Pharisees in that they did not accept the idea of a bodily resurrection after death. However, the Sadducees joined with the Pharisees against Jesus because he criticised them and they saw him as a threat to their relationship with the Romans.

The High Priest

The religious leader of the Jews was the High Priest. He was in charge of the Sanhedrin, the highest Jewish council. Caiaphas was the High Priest at the time of Jesus' death.

The Zealots

The Zealots were a group of Jews who used terrorist tactics against the Romans to gain their religious and political freedom. They were passionate about their beliefs and felt strongly that they should have a land of their own. The Zealots refused to pay taxes and used violence against the Romans.

The Samaritans

Samaria lay between Galilee and Judea. The people who lived there, the Samaritans, were a mixed race. They were descended from Jews who had intermarried with foreigners when the Assyrians invaded Israel in the eighth century BC, and so they were only partly Jewish.

The Samaritans worshipped the same God as the Jews and accepted some of their Law. The Gospels show us that there was intense hatred between the Jews and the Samaritans (Luke 19:25–37).

FOR YOUR FOLDER

Copy and complete the following table:

Religious Groups	Key Points
Pharisees	
Sadducees	
High Priest	
Scribes	
Zealots	
Samaritans	

Chapter 2

THE IDENTITY OF JESUS

In this section we will be looking at different events in the life of Jesus that give us some insight into who Jesus claimed to be and what people in first century Palestine thought about him.

TITLES OF JESUS

Throughout the Gospels, the writers use a number of different 'titles' when referring to Jesus. Each tells us something different about the identity of Jesus.

> **TIP**
> As you study the Gospel, make a note of the passages where each of these titles is used. It will be useful to give examples in examination.

Son of God

In the Old Testament the king of Israel was sometimes called God's son (Psalm 2:7) but Jesus never used this title to describe himself. Matthew and Mark use the title 'Son of God' at Jesus' baptism (Matthew 3:13–17, Mark 1:9-13), and his Transfiguration (Matthew 17:1–13, Mark 9:1-8). The title 'Son of God' became a more popular way to describe Jesus after his death and resurrection, and is used widely in the Church today.

Christ – Messiah

The Greek word *christ*, and the Hebrew word *messiah*, both mean 'anointed one'. In the Old Testament the word was used for people who were set aside to carry out a special task. High priests and kings were anointed with oil as a sign that God had chosen them.

The Jews believed that a Messiah would come to save them. Some Jews expected the Messiah to be a prophet, like Moses. Others expected a military Messiah who would drive out the Romans and set up a kingdom on Earth for them, restoring the glory of the reign of King David.

Jesus never referred to himself as 'Messiah'. Rather than a powerful military leader, Jesus seems to identify himself with Isaiah's prophecy of a 'suffering servant' (Isaiah 52:13–53:12). When the disciple Peter describes Jesus as the Messiah (Matthew 16:16), he accepts it, but warns the disciples to tell no one.

At various points in the Gospels, the writers make it very clear to the reader that Jesus is the Messiah. Examples include: Jesus' baptism (Matthew 3:13–17); Jesus' entry into Jerusalem (Luke 19:28-40); and the trial before the Sanhedrin (Mark 14:53-65).

Son of David

King David (1 Samuel, 2 Samuel and 1 Kings, 1 Chronicles) was regarded as the greatest king of Israel. During his reign Israel was successful and had its own empire. Most Jews expected that their future Messiah would be a descendant of King David, chosen by God to rule as king. Matthew and Luke, the Gospel writers, trace Jesus' family tree back to David. When people used this title for Jesus in the Gospel stories it shows that they believed him to be the Messiah, for example, the healing of the blind man (Matthew 9:27–31).

Son of Man

Jesus often referred to himself using the title 'Son of Man'. This had two meanings:

Firstly, this title was used by the Old Testament prophet Ezekiel to describe himself. He wanted to show that he was an ordinary person. Likewise, Jesus may have called himself 'Son of Man' to remind his disciples that he was a person like them.

Secondly, 'Son of Man' is used in the prophecy of Daniel 7:13 to describe a figure with authority from God. Many people connected this prophecy with the idea of the coming Messiah.

Jesus used the title 'Son of Man' when he talked about his ministry on earth, when he was talking about his death, and when he spoke about his ascension into heaven.

Saviour

'Jesus' means 'God saves'. The Jews expected a military Messiah who would overthrow their enemies. However, Jesus as Saviour means something else for Christians. Christians believe that Jesus offers salvation to humankind (saves them) through his death and resurrection. This means that Jesus sacrificed himself and took the punishment that was due to humankind.

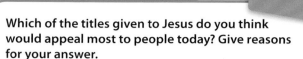

FOR YOUR FOLDER

Which of the titles given to Jesus do you think would appeal most to people today? Give reasons for your answer.

KEY EVENTS SURROUNDING THE BIRTH OF JESUS

The Birth of Jesus is Announced

LUKE 1:26–45

Luke describes how Mary found out that she was going to give birth to the future Messiah. This event is known as the *Annunciation*. The angel announced four things to Mary:

1. that she will conceive a son.
2. that he will be called Jesus.
3. that he will be great, the Son of God.
4. that he will sit on the throne of David forever – a reference to Jesus' identity as the Messiah.

Mary and Joseph were not yet married, but engaged. Engagement at the time of Jesus was considered to be a very serious commitment. Engagements were very rarely broken off. However, as they were not married, and had not had sex, it was a huge shock for Mary to find out that she was pregnant.

Mary was stunned by this news and asked the angel how it could be possible, since she was a virgin. The angel explained that the child would be conceived by the Holy Spirit. Mary showed that she was willing for this to take place.

Mary visited her relative Elizabeth, to tell her the good news. Elizabeth was also pregnant – her child would later be known as John the Baptist. When Mary arrived, Elizabeth felt her unborn child move within her. This may be a sign that John, even before his birth, recognised Jesus' greatness. Elizabeth, filled with the Holy Spirit, seems to know what Mary has been told, and calls her *"my Lord's Mother"* (Luke 1:43).

Joseph's Reaction
MATTHEW 1:18–24

Joseph must have been horrified when he heard that Mary was pregnant. He probably assumed that she had slept with another man. Such behaviour was punishable by death according to the Jewish law. We can see that Joseph was a kind man because he planned to break off the engagement privately rather than draw unwelcome attention to Mary.

However, Joseph was persuaded to change his mind through a dream where an angel explained to him that Mary's pregnancy was not the result of unfaithfulness on her part, but that the baby had in fact been conceived by the Holy Spirit. The miraculous birth of Jesus is referred to as the 'Virgin Birth'.

NOTE

THE IMPORTANCE OF THE VIRGIN BIRTH
The Gospels tell us that Mary was a virgin when Jesus was born. Matthew explains that these events fulfil the prophecy: *"A virgin will become pregnant and have a son, and he will be called Immanuel"* (Isaiah 7:14).

FURTHER THINKING

Mary is an important figure in the Catholic Church. Find out what Catholics believe about the following aspects of Mary's life:

Divine Motherhood   Perpetual Virgin

Immaculate Conception   Assumption

IN A GROUP

1. Why do you think some people find it difficult to accept the miracle of the virgin birth?

2. Why do you think Mary was so stunned by the angel's news?

3. How was the miracle of Jesus' conception confirmed, when Mary visited Elizabeth?

The Birth of Jesus
LUKE 2:120

In these verses, Luke stresses the link between Jesus and King David from the Jewish Scriptures. David came from Bethlehem and Luke describes how Joseph, a descendant of David, had to return there for a census. This is important because it had been prophesied that the ruler over Israel would come from Bethlehem (Micah 5:2).

NOTE

WHAT IS A CENSUS?
A census is a record of the people living in a land. In Northern Ireland a census is carried out every ten years. Forms are sent to each household. Details of a census would include names, ages, and perhaps occupations of everyone living in the house at the time.

Shepherds, at the time of Jesus, were outcasts. They spent most of their lives alone, wandering the fields with their sheep. They had a bad reputation for stealing – grazing sheep on land that wasn't theirs. They would have smelled bad, and their work meant that they would have been unable to carry out their Jewish religious duties.

It was to these outcasts that the news of the Messiah's birth was given – a sign that this Messiah was for everyone, even the poor and marginalised.

The shepherds were terrified by the presence of the angel. They were told that a Saviour had been born in Bethlehem. An army of angels appeared, singing praises to God:

"Glory to God in the highest heaven, and peace on earth to those with whom he is pleased."
(Luke 2:14)

The Christian Church remembers the song of the angels in a hymn known as the *Gloria in Excelsis*, which you may have heard sung by choirs at Christmas time.

The Shepherds found the baby as the angel described, lying in a feeding trough. Though Jesus was 'Messiah', his birth was humble. He was not going to be the kind of king or ruler that people expected the Messiah to be.

Visitors from the East   MATTHEW 2:1–12

The next instalment in the story is recorded by Matthew, and takes place a few months after the birth of Jesus.

Many traditions and stories have grown up around these mysterious visitors. Most people picture them as three wealthy kings who wore the finest of clothes and arrived in the stable alongside the shepherds. You only have to look at a typical nativity set to picture the scene. However, Matthew does not tell us this.

The visitors from the east are called *Magi*, **wise men**, not kings. We have no idea how many of them there were, only that they carried three gifts. And more importantly, they did not arrive to see Jesus until some weeks or months after his birth. By the time of their visit Mary and Joseph were no longer in the stable but had moved to a house (Matthew 2:11). In the Christian Calendar their visit is celebrated on 6 January and is known as the Feast of the Epiphany.

The wise men have a symbolic role to play in the story of Jesus' birth. Coming from the east, they represent the Gentile (non-Jewish) world coming to worship this new King of the Jews. Jesus had come not just for the Jews but also the Gentiles, and we will see this as the story of Jesus' life unfolds.

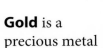

The three gifts brought to Jesus by the visitors from the east are also very symbolic. They represent the type of person Jesus would be during his life:

Gold is a precious metal and represents royalty. It emphasises that Jesus is ruler over the Kingdom of God.

Frankincense was a resin taken from a tree and burned for its smell during Temple worship. It represents Jesus' role as a priest, making a link between God and his people.

Myrrh was oil used to anoint the dead. It represents both Jesus' humanity and his death.

When the visitors from the east had arrived in Jerusalem they had tried to get Herod's help to find the child. However, Herod was insulted by the suggestion that there was another 'King of the Jews' and wanted to kill him. He pretended that he also wanted to worship the baby and asked the wise men to tell him if they found the child. However, they were warned in a dream of Herod's real intentions and returned home by a different route.

IN A GROUP

Discuss why prophecies from Jewish Scripture might have been used in the gospel accounts of Jesus' birth.

In the stories about the birth of Jesus, God spoke through visions and dreams. Do you think God still speaks to people like this today? Give reasons for your answer.

"People today have forgotten the religious significance of Christmas." Do you agree or disagree? Give reasons for your answer.

NOTE

INCARNATION
Jesus' birth is described as an 'incarnation' which means God coming to earth and taking on human form as a man. It literally means 'becoming flesh'.

FOR YOUR FOLDER

1. Who asked 'Where is the baby born to be the King of the Jews?'

2. Why was Herod upset by the visit of the men from the east?

3. Why was it important that Jesus was born in Bethlehem?

4. Explain the significance of the gifts brought by the visitors from the east.

5. What role did angels play at the birth of Jesus?

6. Explain the meaning of the following terms:

   Incarnation   Virgin birth

   Immaculate Conception

JESUS' BAPTISM AND TEMPTATIONS

The Baptism of Jesus   MATTHEW 3:1–17

The baptism of Jesus by John the Baptist is recorded in all four Gospels. Matthew describes John the Baptist like an ancient Jewish prophet. We usually imagine a prophet to be someone who makes predictions about the future, but in the Bible a prophet was a person who explained the implications of God's word for the present day.

Prophets were not always popular people. They were often outspoken and offended people with their message. Likewise, John the Baptist called the religious leaders 'snakes' and said they were like trees which would be cut down and thrown into a fire.

Matthew believed that John was just like the prophet Elijah, that he was a second Elijah. We can see this later on in the words of Matthew 17:12–13:

"'But I tell you that Elijah has already come and people did not recognise him, but treated him just as they pleased.' In the same way they will also ill-treat the Son of Man.' Then the disciples understood that he was talking to them about John the Baptist."

Another clue that John was a second Elijah was the way he looked. He dressed almost exactly like Elijah:

"He was wearing a cloak made of animal skins, tied with a leather belt,' they answered. 'It's Elijah!' the king exclaimed" (2 Kings 1:8).

"John's clothes were made of camel's hair; he wore a leather belt around his waist and his food was locusts and wild honey" (Matthew 3:4).

John's role was to announce the Messiah.

"John was the man the prophet Isaiah was talking about when he said: "Someone is shouting in the desert, 'Prepare a road for the Lord; make a straight path for him to travel!'" (Matthew 3:3, see Isaiah 40:3).

John fulfils this prophecy, living in the desert wilderness of Judea and preaching. People came to him to be baptised in the river Jordan.

Baptism was not a new idea. Being ritually cleansed by total immersion in water was a Jewish ritual. John baptised people as a sign of *repentance* – a way of saying sorry to God and making a fresh start in life.

"At that time Jesus arrived from Galilee and came to John at the Jordan to be baptised by him" (Matthew 3:13).

At first John was reluctant to baptise Jesus because he did not feel that he was worthy or good enough to do the job. He also believed that as Jesus was perfect he did not need to repent of sin. Eventually he agreed and the baptism took place. It was accompanied by three important events, which were signs of God's presence:

1. The heavens opened
2. The Spirit of God appeared
3. A voice from heaven spoke

The Spirit of God *"descended like a dove"* (Matthew 3:16). The voice from heaven (Matthew 3:17) quoted from Psalm 2:7 and Isaiah 42:1, confirming Jesus' divine identity.

FOR YOUR FOLDER

1. How could John the Baptist be compared to the prophet Elijah?

2. Why do you think John was reluctant to baptise Jesus?

3. What three important events occurred as Jesus was baptised?

4. Why do you think Jesus was baptised?

5. Do you think it is necessary for Christians to be baptised?

The Temptations of Jesus   MATTHEW 4:1–11

After Jesus was baptised he took some time to think about what had happened and what was ahead of him in his life. It was important for Jesus to think about how he would use his power to teach people about the Kingdom of God. Matthew tells us that he spent forty days in the desert during which he was tempted by the devil.

Some people picture the devil as an evil little red man with horns and a tail. However, most Christians regard the temptations that Jesus faced as a mental and spiritual struggle. Faced with each temptation, Jesus had to choose the difficult path, turning his back on the easy options which would have led him to evil.

The three temptations Jesus faces in Matthew's Gospel give us insight into the sort of issues that Jesus was wrestling with during his forty days in the desert.

1. **'Order these stones to turn into bread'**
   The first temptation Jesus faced questioned his ability to perform miracles, and tempted him to use his power selfishly.

   Jesus denied himself the chance to satisfy his hunger, even though he had been fasting and would have been starving. Many people would have been impressed by a miracle that would satisfy their physical hunger, but they would not be following him for his teaching.

   Jesus responds quoting Deuteronomy 8:3, showing that he was not concerned with material things like food for the body, but with spiritual food given by God.

2. **'Throw yourself down'**
   In the second temptation Jesus was told to throw himself from the Temple, so that the angels would rescue him. On this occasion the devil quoted scripture (Psalm 91:11–12). He wanted Jesus to misuse his power in order to prove that he was the Messiah and to prove that God loved him. If Jesus carried out spectacular miracles like this he would attract large crowds but they may not have listened to his teaching. Miracles were to be the result of faith in Jesus. Jesus responded to the devil with another quotation from scripture (Deuteronomy 6:16).

3. **'Kneel down and worship me'**

This was a test to see if Jesus would use evil powers to achieve his mission. Would he be able to refuse the chance to have power over the whole earth? Jesus' response to this third temptation shows that he did not see the Messiah as a military or political leader that many Jews expected, but someone who was prepared to put God's kingdom first. Again Jesus used scripture in his response to the devil (Deuteronomy 6:13).

Jesus' response shows that he succeeded in fighting against temptation. He was completely obedient to the will of God, even in the face of suffering. Jesus was now prepared to begin his ministry.

FURTHER THINKING

The season of Lent is linked to the story of Jesus' temptations. Find out why. What do Christians today do during the season of Lent?

IN A GROUP

1. Make a list of ways in which teenagers are tempted today.

2. Do you think that having a religious faith helps a person to deal with temptation?

3. "If God will always forgive, then you can give in to temptation and do what you want". Do you agree or disagree?

FOR YOUR FOLDER

1. Describe each of the temptations of Jesus in the wilderness.

2. Why do you think Jesus was tempted?

3. To which temptation did Jesus respond 'Do not put the Lord your God to the test'?

4. How can Christians learn from Jesus' response to temptation?

5. Jesus' responses to the three temptations all came in the form of quotations from the Jewish Scriptures. They were originally commands given to the nation of Israel by God after their escape from Egypt.

Look them up for yourself, copy out the following table, and enter them in the space provided:

Temptation	Scripture used by Jesus	What does it say?
	Deuteronomy 8:3	
	Deuteronomy 6:16	
	Deuteronomy 6:13	

PETER'S DECLARATION OF FAITH

MATTHEW 16:13–20

An important event took place at Caesarea Philippi which revealed Jesus as the promised Messiah. Jesus openly asked his disciples about his identity. His first question, *"Who do people say the Son of man is?"* (Matthew 16:13) shows us what the general Jewish public thought: that the Son of Man was John the Baptist, Elijah, Jeremiah or some other prophet.

Caesarea Philippi

Jesus' second question was directed at his disciples: *"Who do you say that I am?"* (Matthew 16:15). Peter, who was one of Jesus' closest disciples, was very clear about his opinion: *"You are the Messiah, the Son of the living God"* (Matthew 16:16).

Jesus then ordered the disciples not to tell anyone about what had happened.

FOR YOUR FOLDER

1. Explain the meaning of the words *christ* and *messiah*.

2. Give an account of Peter's declaration about Jesus.

3. Why do you think it is important for Christians that Jesus was identified as the 'Christ' and not just a good man?

THE TRANSFIGURATION
MATTHEW 17:1–9

Six days after Peter confessed that Jesus was *"the Messiah, the Son of the Living God"* (Matthew 16:16), a dramatic event called the Transfiguration took place. There are three important things to note:

1. The change in Jesus' appearance:
The word **transfigured** means to be transformed or to change appearance, making something more spiritual or important. At the Transfiguration, Jesus' appearance was changed by becoming *"like the sun"* (Matthew 17:2).

2. The presence of Moses and Elijah:
Jesus was shown to be equal to the two most important figures in Judaism: Moses and Elijah.

Moses represented the **Law**
Elijah represented the **Prophets**

The Law and the Prophets are the foundation of Jewish religion. The appearance of Moses and Elijah communicates that Jesus fulfilled their prophecies, and his teaching fulfilled the Law.

It was believed that figures from the scriptures would appear in the lead up to the end of the world.

3. The cloud and the voice:
A shining cloud also came from above and a voice spoke from the cloud, confirming that Jesus was the Son of God. In the Old Testament a cloud was a symbol of God's presence (Exodus 24:15–18; 40:34). The words spoken were similar to those at Jesus' baptism (see page 17).

Peter suggested marking the place where the Transfiguration had taken place by building three tents for Jesus, Moses and Elijah. This was a Jewish custom to remember the great figures of Judaism. Jews today still celebrate the 'Feast of Tabernacles'.

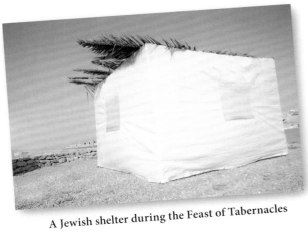
A Jewish shelter during the Feast of Tabernacles

Jesus warned the disciples not to tell anyone about the Transfiguration until the Son of Man (Jesus) had risen from the dead. This is similar to the occasions when Jesus told people not to tell others about his miracles. There would come a time, after his death, when the significance of the Transfiguration would be understood.

FOR YOUR FOLDER

1. Name the characters from Jewish Scripture who appeared with Jesus at the Transfiguration and explain their significance.

2. Name another occasion when God said he was pleased with Jesus.

3. Why do you think the Transfiguration was important for the disciples?

Chapter 3

THE TEACHING OF JESUS

Jesus was a teacher (a rabbi) who tried to get God's message across to the ordinary people. His teaching can be described as being both practical and challenging and he used relevant stories and themes to keep his audiences interested. Jesus' teaching was not only relevant for the first century but can also be applied to life in the twenty-first century.

DISCIPLES
All rabbis or teachers in Jesus' day had disciples who learned from their teaching and tried to follow in their footsteps. Jesus was no exception. He had twelve close followers, or disciples, who helped him in his ministry.

A disciple is a follower or a learner. For example, in the world of work, a person might be a trainee mechanic who learns his trade from a fully qualified mechanic. This is called an apprenticeship.

THE IMPLICATIONS OF DISCIPLESHIP
MATTHEW 8:18–22

A teacher of the law told Jesus that he would follow Jesus wherever he went. Jesus told him: *"Foxes have holes, and birds have nests, but the Son of Man has nowhere to lie down and rest"* (Matthew 8:20). Jesus explains that he lives a homeless life. If the teacher of the law follows him, he would be homeless as well.

Another man told Jesus that he would follow him after he buried his father. Jesus replies *"let the dead bury their own dead"* (Matthew 8:22). This may seem harsh, but Jesus was stressing that discipleship must take priority over everything. Jesus' disciples made sacrifices to follow him.

To be a Christian today also requires sacrifice. Some of the sacrifices a person might have to make in committing to Christianity include the following:

Attitudes towards money and possessions
"Can you have a lot of money and be a Christian?"

Service to others
"What should I be do to help others?"

Friendships
"Who am I spending my time with?"

Priorities
"What are the most important things in my life?"

Popularity

"Am I prepared to give up my popularity?"

Comfortable lifestyle

"I have a great lifestyle. I'm not prepared to make any changes to follow Christ."

FURTHER THINKING

What sacrifices might someone have to make if they followed Christ?

The Mission of the Twelve   MATTHEW 10:9–14

The mission of the twelve marked a new stage in Jesus' ministry. The disciples were invited to join in Jesus' mission.

The event is described in all three Synoptic Gospels, although Matthew's account is more detailed than those of Mark and Luke. It describes how the twelve disciples were sent out by Jesus to do what they had seen Jesus do. They were sent out in pairs to spread the good news that *"The Kingdom of Heaven is near"* (Matthew 10:7). Jesus gave them authority and power to cast out evil spirits and to heal the sick. The mission of the disciples is an extension of the mission of Jesus.

There were two main reasons why the disciples were sent out in pairs:

1. For protection – the roads would have been dangerous for a man to travel on his own.

2. It was accepted that the evidence of two witnesses could be trusted (Deuteronomy 17:6).

The disciples were given some further instructions. They were to travel light and rely on the hospitality of people who took them in. By doing so the disciples would show that they completely relied on God for everything that they would need. Being a disciple of Jesus means learning to depend on God rather then yourself.

Jesus expected his disciples to face rejection as well as acceptance. If the disciples were not welcomed in a town, they were told to shake the dust from their feet as they left – a warning to people that they had rejected God.   Normally, Jews would shake the dust from their feet when leaving a Gentile area. For a Jew to give this symbolic gesture to another Jew was a very serious action.

NOTE

AN EXAMPLE OF MISSION IN ACTION:
Mother Teresa became a Loretto nun when she was 17 years old. She trained in Dublin and then went to Calcutta in India, where she taught in a school. She was very concerned about the amount of poverty she saw on the streets of India. She got permission from the Pope to go to help the poor. In 1950 she was allowed to form a new order and invited other nuns to come and join her in her work.

FURTHER THINKING

1. Find out how Mother Teresa spent the rest of her life from 1950 onwards.

2. Why do you think Mother Teresa helped the elderly, sick and poor?

3. What can other Christians learn from the work of Mother Teresa?

IN A GROUP

1. Have you ever come across people who work in pairs to spread their beliefs? Perhaps someone has called to your house or gives out leaflets in your town centre. How are these people treated by those that they meet?

2. What do you think of their methods of spreading their beliefs?

3. Can you think of other ways that people can share their faith in the twenty-first century?

4. Do you think that the Church today has a role to play in healing the sick?

FOR YOUR FOLDER

1. What did Jesus suggest that his followers should be prepared to do?

2. What advice did Jesus give to the twelve disciples when he sent them out on mission?

3. How were the disciples sent out and what authority did Jesus give them?

4. "Being a disciple of Jesus is difficult in the twenty-first century." Do you agree or disagree? Give reasons for your answer.

THE NEW COVENANT

The religion of the Jewish people was centered on a covenant or agreement between God and Moses. God freed the people of Israel from slavery in Egypt. God spoke to this brand new nation at Mount Sinai, and gave them the Ten Commandments and a new law to live by. The law was recorded in the books of Exodus, Leviticus and Deuteronomy.

When Jesus came, this Old Covenant was updated. Jesus believed that the outward keeping of the law was not enough to please God. Instead Jesus stresses the importance of a person's attitude, as well as a person's actions.

Jesus' teaching in Matthew Chapters 5–7 is known as The Sermon on the Mount. Just as Moses received the Ten Commandments on a mountain, Matthew shows Jesus on a mountain, teaching on their true meaning. Jesus gave examples of Jewish teaching given by Moses and explained what they meant. God's Covenant with Moses is compared with Jesus' New Covenant.

JESUS' TEACHING ON PRAYER

How not to Pray
MATTHEW 6:5–8

Jesus began his teaching on prayer by saying how not to pray:

'Don't show off'

Synagogues were places of worship where Jews gathered to pray. It was not unusual to hear people praying loudly just so they could be seen by others. Jesus was not impressed by this. He called such people **hypocrites**. A hypocrite is a person whose words and actions contradict each other.

Jesus teaches his followers to pray for the right reasons. It doesn't matter if they are on their own or in a public gathering, such as a church service. They are not praying simply to be seen and praised by others.

'Don't use a lot of meaningless words'

The Gentiles' prayers were long because they thought that this practice would impress their many gods. Jesus taught that his followers did not need to be like that because God knows what they need before they ask.

FOR YOUR FOLDER

1. Make a list of occasions when people pray.

2. Do you pray? Can you think of a time when praying helped you?

The Parable of the Pharisee and the Tax Collector
LUKE 18:9–14

Jesus told a parable about a Pharisee and a tax collector.

Pharisees were a group of religious leaders who were strict about keeping the law and went to great efforts to be seen as very religious. They fasted twice a week, even though the law only required fasting once a year on the Day of Atonement. They paid tithes (one tenth) on everything, even though it was not necessary. Many Jews looked up to the Pharisees and admired them.

Tax collectors, on the other hand, were despised in Jewish society. They worked for the Romans and were well known for stealing from the ordinary people by taking too much tax and keeping some for themselves.

In this parable the Pharisee and the tax collector were both praying at the Temple.

The Pharisee prayed to God, thanking him that he was so much better than other people – that he was not greedy, dishonest or an adulterer. He even commented that he was better than the tax collector standing nearby.

The tax collector was so ashamed that he could not even lift his head. Instead he begged God to have pity on him and described himself as a sinner. Jesus shocked his listeners by telling them that it was the tax collector and not the Pharisee who was right with God. The tax collector was truly sorry for his sins. Jesus pointed out the importance of being humble:

> "For all who make themselves great will be humbled, and all who humble themselves will be made great" (Luke 18:14).

This parable shows that God welcomes wrongdoers who admit their need to be forgiven. Those who are self-righteous, who think they are better than everyone else and do not see their own need to be forgiven, are not right with God.

IN A GROUP

What would the Parable of the Pharisee and the tax collector be like if Jesus told it today?

What kind of person would take the place of the religious Pharisee? Who would be the hated tax collector?

Retell the parable of the Pharisee and the tax collector in a modern setting.

Act out your story for the rest of the class to see.

FOR YOUR FOLDER

1. Give an account of the parable of the Pharisee and the tax collector.
2. Explain the differences in their prayers.
3. What relevance does this parable have for Christians today?

NOTE

WHAT IS A PARABLE?

A parable is a story that illustrates a spiritual truth about the Kingdom of God. Jesus used parables to teach his followers.

Jesus' disciples asked him why he used parables when he talked to people. Jesus explained that through parables those who wanted to know more about God's kingdom would progress to understand more. Those who had closed their minds and their hearts to God would never understand even a little.

They were a common method used by many teachers or rabbis at that time.

Jesus used everyday situations in his parables. It showed the people that he was on their level and understood their lives.

Jesus used parables to teach the people for the following reasons:

Parables challenged people to work out the meaning for themselves. People would have enjoyed listening and trying to discover the hidden meaning.

A parable was easy to understand.

JESUS' TEACHING ON FORGIVENESS

Revenge
MATTHEW 5:38–42

Seeking revenge was acceptable under the Old Covenant. The law of retaliation said: *"An eye for an eye and a tooth for a tooth"* (Exodus 21:24). The purpose of this was to limit revenge. So if someone knocked out your tooth, you could knock out their tooth and nothing more. By the time of Jesus this was no longer taken literally, however money was used instead. So if someone wronged you, then you were entitled to sue them.

Jesus taught that all revenge was wrong. He taught his followers that they should 'turn the other cheek', even if severely provoked by someone. In practice this meant being good, even to people who treat you badly. Jesus may have been teaching his followers to shame those who wronged them into doing the right thing.

FOR YOUR FOLDER

Complete Jesus' instructions to his followers regarding revenge:

1. If someone slaps you on the right cheek…

2. If someone takes you to court to sue you for your shirt…

3. If one of the occupation troops forces you to carry his pack one kilometre…

Love for Enemies
MATTHEW 5:42–48

The command to *"love your neighbour as you love yourself"* comes from Leviticus 19:18. Over time it had turned into a saying, 'Love your neighbour and hate your enemies'. However, the phrase 'and hate your enemies' is not found in scripture. The people had interpreted this to mean that they should love fellow Jews but that they ought to hate their enemies.

Jesus told his followers to *"love your enemies and pray for those who persecute you"* (Matthew 5:44). There is nothing particularly difficult about loving your friends. In fact, that is easy to do (see Matthew 5:47). Loving enemies was a radical new idea that would have shocked Jesus' listeners. How could they love or pray for the Romans who occupied their land and often treated them badly?

Martin Luther King attempted to put Jesus' teachings from the Sermon on the Mount into practice in his own life. He led the American Civil Rights campaign during the 1960s, which tried to achieve equality for black Americans.

Although his protest brought him into confrontation with the authorities he always insisted that his followers acted in a non-violent way. They participated in forms of protest such as sit-ins or mass meetings which people couldn't ignore but which weren't violent.

Martin Luther King's turn-the-other-cheek policy represented the best way to make his point; to expose the brutality of his opponents and to create a positive, harmonious future.

"Love even for enemies is the key to the solution of the problems of our world – Jesus is not an impractical idealist; he is the practical realist."

"Darkness cannot drive out darkness; only light can do that. Hate cannot drive out hate; only love can do that. Hate multiplies hate, violence multiplies violence and toughness multiplies toughness … so when Jesus says *"Love your enemies"*, he is setting forth a profound and ultimately inescapable admonition."

Reprinted by arrangement with The Heirs to the Estate of Martin Luther King Jr., c/o Writers House as agent for the proprietor New York, NY.

Copyright 1963 Dr. Martin Luther King Jr; copyright renewed 1986 Coretta Scott King

FURTHER THINKING

Do you think people put Jesus teaching to *"love your enemies"* into practice?

What would happen if soldiers in a warzone started following Jesus' teaching to love their enemies?

IN A GROUP

1. Do you think that Jesus' teaching on non-violence is a practical guide for Christian behaviour today?

2. "How you live is more important than what you believe." Do you agree? Give reasons for your opinion.

The Parable of the Unforgiving Servant
MATTHEW 18:21–35

This parable is told in answer to a question about forgiveness. Peter asked Jesus:

> *"Lord, if my brother keeps on sinning against me, how many times do I have to forgive him? Seven?"* (Matthew 18:21)

In Jewish tradition the number seven was a symbol for completeness or perfection. So to forgive seven times would be a gracious act. However, Jesus' reply stressed that forgiveness has no limits:

> *"No, not seven times but seventy times seven."* (Matthew 18:22)

Jesus then went on to explain his answer through a parable: A servant owed a king 'millions of pounds' which he knew he could never repay even if he was sold as a slave, along with his wife and family. The servant went to the king and promised the impossible: to repay the king everything. The king felt sorry for him because he knew that this was

impossible, and so he cancelled the debt. The fact that the debt was so big shows the extent of the king's forgiveness.

However, the forgiven servant quickly forgot how forgiving the king had been. When the servant met a fellow servant who could not repay a debt he refused to be patient with him and threw him into jail. The first servant failed to learn from the king's example. When the king heard this he was outraged and immediately withdrew his forgiveness from the unforgiving servant. He put the first servant into jail until he paid back his own debt.

The parable means that because Christians have been forgiven so much themselves, then they must never be unwilling to forgive others.

FOR YOUR FOLDER

1. How many times did Peter think a person should be forgiven?

2. How many times did Jesus say a person should be forgiven?

3. Retell the parable of the Unforgiving Servant in your own words.

4. "A Christian should always forgive no matter what the situation." Do you agree or disagree? Give reasons for your answer showing you have considered different points of view.

IN A GROUP

Look in newspaper and magazine articles for crimes against people. Group stories into those you could easily forgive and those that you would have difficulty in forgiving.

Look at the group of stories where you think forgiveness is difficult and discuss the following questions;

What effects does not forgiving have on communities of people?

Why is it important for communities to try to live in harmony *(community cohesion)*?

Is Jesus' teaching on forgiveness practical for community cohesion?

FURTHER THINKING

Find out what you can about *Gordon Wilson*. His daughter, Marie, was one of eleven people killed in an IRA bomb in Enniskillen in 1987.

IN A GROUP

What do you think it would be like to win the lottery? Would you tell people? What would you do with the money? Would you still live in the same house or town? Would you give money to your friends? Who would you give money to? How much would you give away? Where would you draw the line? Think about how your life would change. Would you be happier than you are now?

JESUS' TEACHING ON WEALTH AND POVERTY

How important is money to you? Do you have a part-time job? Do you get money for babysitting or doing chores around the house? Are you lucky enough to get pocket money? Look at the following pie-chart. Draw a similar one using the pupils in your class to show how your class spends money. Some suggestions are:

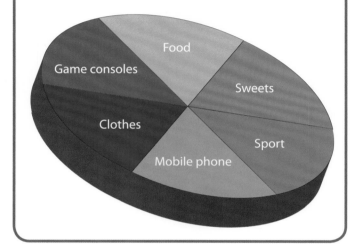

Teaching about Charity   MATTHEW 6:1–4

At the time of Jesus religious duties involved charity, prayer and fasting. Jesus taught that those who carry out these duties to gain a good reputation get exactly that – but nothing more. He pointed out that *"they have already been paid in full"* (Matthew 6:2). Jesus called such people hypocrites. Religious people were giving money to charity which is a kind and humble thing to do, yet they were proud and boastful about the way that they did it. Instead Jesus taught that Christians should give to the needy in such a way that only God knows about it. Then they would be rewarded appropriately.

Look back at the pie-chart you made in your class. Did anyone consider giving to charity as part of it? Christians believe that giving to charity is very important, no matter how much money you have. There are many ways to give privately to charity. Can you make a list?

Red Nose Day is a UK-wide fundraising event organised by Comic Relief every two years. On Red Nose Day everyone is encouraged to cast inhibitions aside, put on a Red Nose and do something a little bit silly to raise money – celebrities included! It culminates in a night of extraordinary comedy and moving documentary films on BBC One.

It's an event that unites the entire nation in trying to make a difference to the lives of thousands of people, both across Africa and in the UK, who face terrible injustice or who live in abject poverty.

Find out more at www.rednoseday.com

God and Possessions
MATTHEW 6:24–34

Jesus used the image of a slave to talk about how people can be obsessed by money. Jesus also challenged his listeners about what was most important to them: *"You cannot serve both God and money"* (Matthew 6:24).

Today, people are continually faced with the pressure to have more: the latest gadget, a flashy car, a big house, and impressive job… Jesus taught that the Kingdom of God is more important than money or possessions, and that his followers should not even worry about their clothes, or where their next meal is coming from.

He used examples from the natural world to get his point across: birds don't store up food like people do, yet they find food and are taken care of; wild flowers don't have to worry about what they are wearing, yet they are beautiful.

Jesus taught that Christians should not worry about money and possessions because God would provide them with everything that they need.

FOR YOUR FOLDER

1. What were Jesus' instructions about giving to others?

2. What did Jesus teach about 'worry'?

3. How did Jesus use the symbolism of 'birds' and 'wild flowers' to make a point?

4. Discuss what comfort a Christian might get from Matthew 6:24–34?

FURTHER THINKING

Research:

Go to your local library or search the Internet to find out about the work of a charity. Write a short report to include five key points about the charity. Report back to the rest of the class.

THE PARABLE OF THE SOWER
MATTHEW 13:1–9, 18–23

The Parable of the Sower is a clear example of a parable or allegory about the Kingdom of God. It is one of the most famous parables told by Jesus.

Matthew writes about this parable in three parts:

- **Chapter 13:1–9:**
The Parable of the Sower, which Jesus told to a large crowd

- **Chapter 13:10–17*:**
Jesus explains the purpose of parables to his disciples

- **Chapter 13:18–23:**
Jesus explains the parable of the sower to his disciples

As well as having meaning for the listeners of Jesus' day the parable of the Sower has a clear message for people today. The following diagram explains the meaning of the Parable of the Sower:

THE PARABLE	MEANING	SIGNIFICANCE FOR TODAY
"Once there was a man who went out to sow corn." (13:3)	**Man** God **Seed** The Word of God	The parable teaches what will happen when the Word of God is proclaimed. The Word of God is like seed which is planted and starts to grow. If people listen to God's word they will grow in a spiritual way.
"As he scattered the seed in the field some of it fell along the path and the birds ate it up." (13:4)	**Path** "Those who hear the message about the Kingdom but do not understand it." (13:19) **Birds** "The Evil One comes along and snatches away what was sown in them." (13:19)	Some people are distracted from taking the Christian faith seriously. Can you think of some things that might distract people?
"Some of it fell on the rocky ground, where there was little soil. The seeds soon sprouted, because the soil wasn't deep. But when the sun came up, it burnt the young plants; and because the roots had not grown deep enough, the plants soon dried up." (13:5–6)	**Rocky ground** "Those who receive the message gladly as soon as they hear it. But it does not sink deep into them, and they don't last long." (13:20–21) **Sun** "So when trouble or persecution comes along because of the message, they give up at once." (13:22)	Some people are attracted by Christianity until they realise what it means to be a Christian, that it requires a deep commitment. **What sort of changes might someone have to make to be a Christian?**
"Some of the seed fell among the thorn bushes, which grew up and choked the plants." (13:7)	**Thorn bushes** "Those who hear the message; but the worries about life and the love for riches choke the message and they don't bear fruit." (13:22)	Some people let worries ruin God's influence on their lives. **What sort of worries might they have?** The 'thorns' can be compared to greed, anger or jealousy, all of which choke spiritual growth.
"But some seed fell in good soil, and the plants produced corn, some produced a hundred grains, others sixty, and others thirty." (v13:8)	**Good soil** "Those who hear the message and understand it: they bear fruit, some as much as a hundred, others sixty, others thirty." (13:23)	A few people will accept the Gospel message and stay firm in their faith, in spite of difficulties which they may face. They will continue to grow as Christians, carrying out God's purpose in their lives.

IN A GROUP

Discuss the different ways in which people respond to the Gospel message today.
What distractions prevent people from becoming Christians?

*not on GCSE course

Chapter 4

THE DEEDS OF JESUS

Jesus was not just a man of words. He put his own teachings into action by how he lived.
In this section we will look at how he dealt with those viewed as outcasts by society, his relationship with women, and how his teachings and lifestyle caused controversy with Religious leaders.

JESUS' DEALINGS WITH RELIGIOUS LEADERS
MATTHEW 23:1–12, 23–28

Jesus warns his listeners against the Teachers of the Law and the Pharisees. He criticises them harshly, calling them hypocrites – People who say one thing, but do another: *"They don't practise what they preach"* (Matthew 23:3).

Jesus gives two instructions to his followers:

1. To do what the Scribes and Pharisees tell them to do, because they are the authorised interpreters of the Law of Moses.

2. Not to follow the example of the Scribes and Pharisees because they say one thing and do another.

Jesus then gives some specific criticisms of the scribes and Pharisees:

"Look at the straps with scripture verses on them which they wear on their foreheads and arms, notice how large they are! Notice how long are the tassels on their cloaks" (Matthew 23:5).

Phylacteries, or *Tefillin*, are small wooden or leather boxes that are strapped to a person's forehead or left arm. Each box holds strips of parchment inscribed with passages from the Jewish scriptures.

Tefillin are worn in response to Deuteronomy 6:6–8: *"Never forget these commands that I am giving you today. Teach them to your children. Repeat them when you are at home and when you are away, when you are resting and when you are working. Tie them on your arms and wear them on your foreheads as a reminder."*

Another tradition was to wear a shawl with tassels called a *Tallit*. The shawl was used to cover the head for prayer, or when performing religious duties. Some of the scribes and Pharisees wore these all the time to look more pious. All of this was done to attract attention and make people think how holy they were.

The *Tallit* is worn in response to Numbers 15:38–40: *"say to the people of Israel: 'Make tassels on the corners of your garments and put a blue cord on each tassel. You are to do this for all time to come. The tassels will serve as reminders, and each time you see them you will remember all my commands and obey them; then you will not turn away from me and follow your own wishes and desires. The tassels will remind you to keep all my commands, and you will belong completely to me.'"*

"They love the best places at feasts and the reserved seats in the synagogues" (Matthew 23:6).

At the time of Jesus seating arrangements at feasts or in the synagogue were determined by how educated or important a person was. In the synagogues the most important seats were on the platform facing the congregation. The Pharisees loved the best seats given to them in public places so that people would know how important they were.

"They love to be greeted with respect in the market place and to be called 'teacher'" (Matthew 23:7).

Jesus condemned the religious leaders for looking to be addressed by flattering titles that would make them seem important.

People would address religious leaders as 'teacher' or 'father'. Jesus said that they should have only one teacher and one father.

"You give to God a tenth even of the seasoning herbs…but you neglect to obey the really important teachings of the Law, such as justice and mercy and honesty" (Matthew 23:23).

The law of Moses stated that one tenth of all the produce of the land should be given to God (Leviticus 27:30). The Pharisees took everything literally and even applied this law to tiny herbs. They made a big fuss of these trivial matters and yet neglected more important issues.

"Blind guides! You strain a fly out of your drink but swallow a camel! " (Matthew 23:24)

If a Pharisee swallowed a dead fly he would become ritually unclean. So the practice of straining wine in order to remove dead insects was common. Jesus opposed such petty rules because they blinded people to the things that really mattered.

"You clean the outside of your cup and plate, while the inside is full of what you have obtained by violence and selfishness…You are like whitewashed tombs, which look fine on the outside but are full of bones and decaying corpses on the inside…" (Matthew 23:25–27)

Both of these criticisms state that the religious leaders appear to be holy and righteous outside, but are corrupt inside.

Jesus summed up his criticisms with the following statement:

"…on the outside you appear good to everybody, but inside you are full of hypocrisy and sin" (Matthew 23:28).

FOR YOUR FOLDER

1. What do we learn from this event about some of the Jewish religious customs?

2. Make a list of the criticisms Jesus had against the Pharisees.

3. Copy out Matthew 23:12 and explain what it means.

4. Sum up in a sentence why Jesus thought the religious leaders were hypocrites.

IN A GROUP

Discuss how religious believers may be called hypocrites today.

JESUS' DEALINGS WITH WOMEN

A Woman's Faith
MATTHEW 15:21–28

On this occasion we get a glimpse into the attitude some people had towards both women and Gentiles. Jesus went into the territory of Tyre, in Phoenicia, which was in the Roman province of Syria (find this on the map on page 5). A woman asked Jesus to cast out an evil spirit from her daughter. News of Jesus' miracles had obviously spread to Gentile areas.

The focus of this story is on the conversation Jesus had with the woman, rather than on the miracle itself. The woman calls Jesus 'Son of David' which shows that she knew exactly who Jesus was. She also calls him 'sir', meaning 'Lord', which was a title for 'God'. At first Jesus ignored the woman, which may seem a strange thing for Jesus to do. Then Jesus seemed to suggest that he had come only for the Jews (Matthew 15:24). The woman persisted because she believed that Jesus could heal her daughter.

Jesus' words to her may seem shocking or even rude:

> *"It isn't right to take the children's food and throw it to the dogs"* (Matthew 15:26).

The term 'dog' was a common description used for Gentiles. The woman's persistence is seen in her clever use of words:

> *"That's true, sir, but even the dogs eat the leftovers that fall from their master's table"* (Matthew 15:27)

Jesus may have been testing this woman's faith, but he was delighted with the results and commended her for her great faith. He healed her daughter and showed that the Kingdom of God is open to everyone.

Women at the time of Jesus were treated as second-class citizens. This woman would have been doubly despised by Jewish men because she was a Gentile. This did not matter to Jesus, who accepted all people equally. The key point is that the gospel is not just for the Jews, but for everyone. This is called 'universalism'.

> UNIVERSALISM is the idea that the Gospel message is for everyone, regardless of race, gender, or religion. No one person is more deserving of the gospel than anyone else.
>
> This would have been a difficult concept for some to accept. They were used to looking down upon women, Gentiles, and other outcasts.

FOR YOUR FOLDER

1. What opinion did the Gentile woman have of Jesus?

2. Jesus spoke to the woman about dogs feeding from the crumbs that fall from a table. What was he really talking about?

3. What does this miracle teach about 'universalism'?

4. What does this story teach about racism?

Jesus is Anointed at Bethany
MARK 14:3–9

Jesus was in Bethany at the house of Simon, a healed leper, with his disciples and some others. While Jesus was eating, a woman (John 12:3 says it was Mary, the sister of Lazarus) came to him with an alabaster jar filled with an expensive perfume, which she poured on his head. We know from the account in John's Gospel that the perfume cost about one year's wages (John 12:3–5). The disciples were angry at the apparent waste:

"What was the use of wasting the perfume? It could have been sold for more than three hundred silver coins and the money given to the poor!" (Mark 14:4–5).

There is a sharp contrast between the woman's generosity and the poor attitude of those who criticised her. They failed to appreciate that this anointing of Jesus was symbolic. The word *messiah* means 'anointed one'. A king would be anointed before his coronation, and the dead were anointed before they were buried. The woman's anointing of Jesus was a sign of his coming death.

Jesus defended the woman's actions and used the situation to hint to his disciples what was about to happen: his crucifixion.

"She did what she could; she poured perfume on my body to prepare it ahead of time for burial" (Matthew 14:8).

Jesus then predicted that the woman's anointing would become part of the Gospel story which would be preached in the whole world.

FOR YOUR FOLDER

1. Retell the story of how Jesus was anointed at Bethany.

2. What was the reaction of the disciples to Mary's gesture? Why do you think they felt this way?

3. Explain the meaning of Mary's actions.

The Woman Caught in Adultery JOHN 8:1–11

A woman caught having an affair was brought to Jesus. By Jewish law adultery was punishable by death (Leviticus 20:10; Deuteronomy 22:22). It is interesting to note that the man was also guilty, but he was not brought to Jesus.

The religious leaders remind Jesus that the law demands death by stoning. As a religious teacher himself, they invite Jesus to make the judgement. They were trying to trap him – he would have to either condemn the woman to death, or go against the law.

His judgement outwits the Scribes and the Pharisees:

"Whichever one of you has committed no sin may throw the first stone at her" (John 8:7).

No one in the crowd could meet this request for having no sin in their lives, and one by one they all left. The woman was left alone with Jesus who tells her:

"I do not condemn you either. Go, but do not sin again" (John 8:11).

She leaves unharmed.

Jesus outwitted the religious leaders, taught that it is wrong to judge people, and restored the dignity of the woman, treating her as a human being.

FOR YOUR FOLDER

1. How was adultery viewed in Jewish society?

2. How did the religious leaders try to trick Jesus?

3. Copy out and explain Jesus' words in John 8:7.

4. What was the outcome of this event?

IN A GROUP

1. Some people think that this story allows Christians to behave whatever way they want because they can always ask for forgiveness. What do you think?

2. Discuss what Christians can learn about judging others from this event.

JESUS' DEALINGS WITH A SOCIAL OUTCAST

JOHN 4:1–26

In the story of the Samaritan woman, Jesus crosses both social and religious barriers. On this occasion Jesus was travelling on a mountain road from Judea to Galilee, which involved going through Samaria. It was midday and the sun would have been very hot. He came across a Samaritan woman at a deep well. It would have been unusual for anyone to draw water at midday so perhaps the woman had gone at a time when she would not have to face others, suggesting she was shunned by other women in her community.

Jesus asked the woman for a drink, which was a shocking breach of social custom. It was unheard of for a man to speak to a woman in public, not even their wives. What is even more significant is that she was a Samaritan. The Jews and Samaritans did not mix socially. In fact many Jews regarded the Samaritans as inferior to them (see Chapter 1). The Samaritan woman's surprise at being addressed by Jesus is evident (John 4:9).

Knowing that Jews will not use the same cups as Samaritans, the woman asked Jesus how he could ask someone like her for a drink. He told her that he had asked her for physical water but if she knew who he was she would have asked him for another kind of water. The Jewish Scriptures use the term 'living water' to describe spiritual cleansing and new life that comes through the power of God.

The conversation that followed shows that Jesus knew details of the woman's personal life.

This woman is an outcast on three levels:

1. She is an adulteress
2. She is a woman
3. She is a Samaritan

The woman assumed that Jesus must be a prophet to know so much about her. She tried to change the subject and began to talk about where the Samaritans and Jews worship. Jesus pointed to a time when everyone would worship God in spirit and truth. What followed seemed out of character for Jesus who was usually so careful about revealing his true identity. The woman said that the Messiah would reveal all things and Jesus told her that he was the Messiah (John 4:26).

Here in Samaria Jesus was free to openly declare his identity because he was away from Jewish expectations of what the Messiah should be like.

FOR YOUR FOLDER

1. Describe the relationship between Jews and Samaritans at the time of Jesus.

2. Outline the conversation Jesus had with the Samaritan woman.

3. Copy out and explain the meaning of John 4:13–14

4. Why did the woman say Jesus was a prophet?

5. Why would the disciples have been surprised when they returned?

IN A GROUP

1. Discuss what Jesus' encounters with women teach about universalism.

2. What can Christians learn from Jesus' attitude to women? Use examples in your answer.

3. Some of the Christian denominations allow women to become priests or ministers. Do you think all churches should be more open to this? Give reasons for your answer, showing you have looked at different points of view.

Chapter 5

THE DEATH AND RESURRECTION OF JESUS

Jesus' death was inevitable. However, it still brought immense sadness and distress to his followers. Looking back, Christians can celebrate that because of Jesus' death the offer of salvation is open to all people. It is interesting that Christianity is the only religion that actively celebrates its founder's death. Through Jesus' resurrection he defeated the power of evil and death. Jesus' death and resurrection are central to the Christian faith.

In this section we will look at the events surrounding the death and resurrection of Jesus and consider their significance for the Christians.

THE LAST SUPPER
MATTHEW 26:20–30

Every year Jews celebrate the Passover festival. It remembers the night the Israelites escaped from Egypt where they had been slaves (the Exodus). As Jesus was a Jew, he also celebrated the Passover every year. He had sent his disciples to make sure that everything was ready.

Jesus celebrated the Passover meal along with his disciples. Jesus suddenly announced that he would be betrayed by someone who was sitting at the table with him:

> "One who dips his bread in the dish with me will betray me" (Matthew 26:23).

All of the disciples expressed shock and each of them asked Jesus if they had somehow done something to betray him. Judas asked, *"Surely not me?"*, but at this stage nobody knew who the traitor was because they had all dipped their bread in a common dish.

Jesus pointed out that the traitor would not escape God's judgement:

> "It would have been better for that man if he had never been born" (Matthew 26:24).

What happened next has become the most important ritual for Christians everywhere. Jesus took elements of the Passover meal and made them symbols of his death. Following the usual format of the Passover meal, Jesus blessed the bread, broke it, and passed it around. He did the same with the wine. Jesus explained that the bread was his body and that the wine was his blood, which sealed God's covenant. Just as the previous Covenants between people and God had been sealed with sacrifice, Jesus' death would be the final sacrifice enabling all people to receive God's blessing and forgiveness:

> "This is my blood, which seals God's covenant, my blood poured out for many for the forgiveness of sins" (Matthew 26:28).

In Matthew 26:29 Jesus refers to a time in the future when they would meet again in God's Kingdom.

The Passover or *Seder* meal which Jesus had with his disciples followed a set format:

- An opening prayer and a blessing of the cup
- The dipping of herbs in salt water
- The breaking of unleavened bread
- The reading of the story of the Passover
- The blessing of the second cup
- The festive meal of roast lamb
- The blessing of the third cup

Each item of food on the table symbolised what happened on the night of the first Passover when the Israelites escaped from Egypt. Jews today still celebrate the Passover.

At the Last Supper, Jesus used two of the items on the Passover table to symbolise his own forthcoming death. He took the unleavened bread and said *"this is my body"*. He also took the wine and said *"this is my blood"*. Christians today still remember that night by repeating the actions of eating bread and drinking wine. Different Christian traditions give this act of remembrance different names: Eucharist; Mass; The Lord's Supper; Holy Communion.

DIFFERENT UNDERSTANDINGS OF COMMUNION

Catholic Church

In the Catholic Church the Eucharist or Communion is celebrated daily in the **Mass**. Catholics believe that during the Eucharist the bread and wine change to become the body and blood of Christ. In other words, Christ becomes physically present in the bread and wine. This is known as **transubstantiation**.

Protestant tradition

In most Protestant churches, Communion is regarded as a memorial of Christ's death. The bread and wine do not change at all because they are simply symbols of what Christ has done. Communion means 'sharing' and at a Communion service Christians share together to remember the suffering and death of Christ.

FOR YOUR FOLDER

1. Describe the main events which took place during the Last Supper.

2. What new meaning did Jesus give to the bread and the wine?

3. Explain how Communion is linked to the Passover meal.

IN A GROUP

"The Christian Church places too much emphasis on the sacrament of Communion and not enough on Christian behaviour".
Do you agree or disagree? Give reasons for your answer showing that you have considered different points of view.

JESUS' ARREST
MATTHEW 26:47–56

The disciples went with Jesus to the Garden of Gethsemane, an olive tree plantation. His three closest disciples, Peter and the two sons of Zebedee (James and John), who had been with him at the Transfiguration, went further into the garden with him while he prayed. Jesus told them to 'watch and pray', and even though they probably realised that something momentous was about to happen, they were not able to stay awake.

Judas arrived with the Chief Priests and elders, and an armed crowd to arrest Jesus. In order to make sure the right man was arrested Judas kissed Jesus on the cheek, a common greeting in that culture, and said: *"Peace be with you, Teacher"* (Matthew 26:49). He betrayed Jesus with an act of friendship. This makes Judas' betrayal even worse.

Jesus told Judas: *"Be quick about it friend"* (Matthew 26:50). The rest of the disciples jumped to defend Jesus. One of those with Jesus drew his sword and cut off the ear of the High Priest's slave. Jesus told him to put his sword away and explained that the prophecies must come true. Jesus asks them why they had come to take him by surprise at night, as if he were an outlaw, saying that this also fulfils prophecy.

The disciples were so afraid that they ran away.

FOR YOUR FOLDER

1. How did the disciples let Jesus down in Gethsemane?
2. What did Jesus mean when he said, *"The hour has come"*?
3. Why did Judas kiss Jesus?
4. Why do you think the disciples left Jesus when he was arrested?
5. Do you think it helps if people can talk to God in the same way they approach a loving father? Give reasons for your answer, showing that you have considered other viewpoints.

IN A GROUP

Discuss the following questions:

1. What can Christians learn from the behaviour of the disciples in this story?
2. Explain why Jesus submitted peacefully to his arrest. As the Messiah, what else could he have done?

   As a revision task, look back to the story of Jesus' temptations (Matthew 4:1–11). Remind yourself of the powers that Jesus had.
3. Can you think of any famous Christians whose faith has been tested? What happened and how did they overcome their time of testing?

JESUS' TRIALS

Jesus before the Council
MATTHEW 26:57–68

The Sanhedrin was the official Jewish council or court of justice. It had seventy one members, made up of Pharisees and Sadducees. The head of the council was the High Priest, who at the time of Jesus was Caiaphas.

The council was in control of the affairs of the Jewish people in Palestine. It had most of the powers of a normal court but was not allowed to carry out the death sentence. Only the Romans had the power to put someone to death.

Jesus was brought before the Sanhedrin on a charge of blasphemy, which means speaking in an offensive way about God. There were certain rules that had to be followed for a trial and it seems that Jesus' trial was carried out unfairly. For example:

- A court was not usually held in the High Priest's house. Jesus' trial took place in Caiaphas' house.

- Trials that could result in an execution could not take place at night. Jesus' trial was at night.

- False witnesses could be punished by death. At Jesus' trial two witnesses accused Jesus of threatening to destroy the Temple. (In John 2:19 Jesus told the Jewish authorities that if the Temple was torn down he would have the ability to rebuild it in three days. However, Jesus had not been talking about the real Temple but his body.)

At first Jesus did not answer this accusation, but when he was put under the oath and asked if he was the Messiah he replied: *"So you say"* (Matthew 26:64). Jesus was careful not to agree with the High Priest's us of the word 'messiah', but went on to explain his identity in his own terms:

> *"You will see the Son of Man sitting on the right of the Almighty and coming on the clouds of heaven."*

You will remember that Son of Man is one of the titles that Jesus often used for himself. This time he makes reference to the prophecy of Daniel (Daniel 7:13).

The High Priest had heard enough and tore his robes to express his outrage at such blasphemy. Blasphemy was punishable by death by stoning according to the Jewish law (Leviticus 24:16). The others attacked Jesus, spitting, punching and mocking him.

FOR YOUR FOLDER

1. What was the Sanhedrin?

2. Where was Jesus taken when he was arrested?

3. Explain the meaning of the term 'blasphemy'.

4. What accusation was brought against Jesus about the Temple?

5. Do you think Jesus was right to remain silent when questioned?

6. Why could the Sanhedrin not put Jesus to death?

Jesus before Pilate   MATTHEW 27:1–2, 11-26

Pilate, the Roman Governor, was the only one who could officially sentence Jesus to death so the Jewish leaders handed him over for a second trial. The charge of blasphemy was twisted into a political charge because blasphemy was not a crime under Roman law. By saying that Jesus claimed to be the Messiah the Jewish leaders could argue that he was guilty of leading a rebellion against the Roman Empire.

It is not certain where the trial took place but it may have been in the fortress of Antonia (see plan of the Temple on page 11). Pilate's question to Jesus probably arose out of the Sanhedrin's report that Jesus had claimed to be the Messiah. When Jesus was brought before Pilate he asked him: *"Are you the King of the Jews?"* (Matthew 27:11). If Jesus was claiming to be a king it could be argued that he wanted to rule Palestine and overthrow the Romans.

Jesus did not say anything, which surprised Pilate and gave him no real reason to charge him. Pilate realised that Jesus was a threat to the authority of the Sanhedrin, and they were trying to get rid of him. He was also aware that Jesus was very popular among the ordinary people.

Pilate was clearly uneasy about the case against Jesus and this was confirmed by his wife as a result of a dream. Messages given in dreams were taken very seriously by the Romans. She told Pilate to *"have nothing to do with that innocent man"* (Matthew 27:19). Matthew may have included this conversation in his account because it highlights Jesus' innocence.

In an attempt to find a simple solution, Pilate took the opportunity to use a Passover tradition. Every year the governor could set free one prisoner as a favour to the Jews. At the time there was a well known prisoner called Barabbas who had caused riots and was known to be a dangerous man. Pilate offered the crowd the choice of releasing either Jesus or Barabbas. It seemed obvious that the crowd would ask for Jesus to be released.

Pilate's plan backfired because the Sanhedrin persuaded the crowd to ask for Barabbas, a possible Zealot, to be released instead of Jesus. Clearly Pilate was frustrated at this (Matthew 27:24) and decided to wash his hands of any responsibility for the life of Jesus:

> *"I am not responsible for the death of this man! This is your doing!"* (Matthew 27:24).

He must have felt very uneasy at sentencing a man to death with no real evidence.

Washing one's hands to symbolise innocence was a Jewish custom (Deuteronomy 21:6; Psalm 26:6).

The crowd, so different now from the one that had welcomed Jesus into Jerusalem on Palm Sunday, shouted: *"Let the responsibility for his death fall on us and on our children!"* (Matthew 27:25).

Pilate's job was to maintain Roman rule in Palestine, and that meant keeping good relations with the local leaders. Pilate did what the crowd wanted and sent Jesus to be crucified.

FOR YOUR FOLDER

1. Describe the main features of Jesus' trial before Pilate
2. Explain why Pilate may have had doubts about Jesus' guilt.
3. Why did Pilate wash his hands at Jesus' trial?
4. What can Christians learn from the suffering and behaviour of Jesus at his trials?

JESUS' DEATH
MATTHEW 27:32–61

Crucifixions took place outside the city wall on a hill called *Golgotha* – 'the place of the skull'. Crucifixion was the most extreme form of Roman execution, reserved for the worst criminals, and Jewish scripture described anyone who died by crucifixion as *"under God's curse"* (Deuteronomy 21:22–23). The place of death symbolised rejection by people and by God.

Golgotha: Can you see why it is called the place of the skull?

The Romans crucified people publicly as an example to others. Matthew records that people gathered to watch and even shouted abuse at those condemned. The crowd laughed at Jesus' weakness and reminded him of his claims to have the power of God.

The prophet Isaiah described the Messiah as a suffering servant:

> "He was arrested and led off to die, and no one cared about his fate. He was put to death for the sins of our people" (Isaiah 53:8).

Matthew here presents Jesus as that suffering servant, forsaken and rejected by everyone and yet at the same time, fulfilling the prophecies about the Messiah.

At that time it was not unusual to make a prisoner carry the cross-beam of their own cross to the site of the crucifixion. The fact that Jesus needed the assistance of a man from Cyrene to carry his cross probably shows that he was weak from the torture and beating he had received from the Roman soldiers (Matthew 27:27–31).

The soldiers offered Jesus a drink – a kind of painkiller, which he refused. He was crucified between two criminals. The charge against each criminal would have been written at the top of their cross. In Jesus' case it would have read *IESUS NAZEREUS REX IUDAEORUM* – 'Jesus of Nazareth, King of the Jews'.

FOR YOUR FOLDER

Complete the phrases Jesus was mocked with:

1. *"You were going to tear down the Temple and build it up in three days…"*

2. *"He saved others, but he cannot save himself! Isn't he the king of Israel?..."*

3. *"He trusts in God and claims to be God's Son…"*

Matthew records some strange and amazing things that happened during the last hours of Jesus' life. The whole region was covered in darkness, even though it was the middle of the day. In the Jewish scriptures darkness was often a symbol of tragedy or judgement (Exodus 10:21–23; Amos 8:9–10).

Jesus then called out the words of Psalm 22:1: *"Eli Eli, lema sabacthani"* which means "My God, my God, why did you abandon me?" Some people thought he was calling for the prophet Elijah who, it was believed, would help those in need.

After Jesus had cried out and died there was an earthquake; people rose from the dead and the curtain hanging in the Holy of Holies was torn in two, from top to bottom. Both are symbolic events:

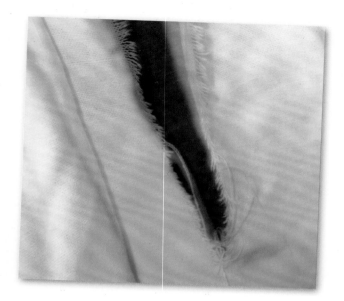

The Holy of Holies was the part of the Temple where the presence of God was said to dwell (see page 10). It was separated from the rest of the temple by a thick curtain. Strict instructions were given concerning the location of this curtain:

"Make a curtain of fine linen woven with blue, purple and red wool. Embroider it with figures of winged creatures. Hang it on four posts of acacia wood covered with gold, fitted with hooks, and set in four silver bases…The curtain will separate the Holy Place from the Most Holy Place" (Exodus 26:31–33).

Only the High Priest could pass through the curtain into God's presence, once a year, having performed complex rituals in preparation.

If the curtain had been torn by human hands the tear would have begun at the bottom. Matthew records that the curtain was torn from "top to bottom" (Matthew 27:51) which suggests that God himself tore the curtain. It has been suggested the destruction of the curtain which symbolically separated people from God represented that the way was open – all people could now come before God. The dead being raised to life represented the future for all those who trusted in Christ's death as a sacrifice which would bring them forgiveness.

It was only after Jesus had died that the soldiers realised that he really was the 'Son of God' (Matthew 27:54) The darkness, earthquake and other supernatural events probably convinced them that this was no ordinary execution.

Jesus was placed in a tomb sealed by a stone and a guard was placed beside it to make sure that the disciples did not steal the body and pretend that Jesus has been resurrected.

FOR YOUR FOLDER

1. Why would the events of the last week of Jesus' life have been a difficult time for the disciples?

2. Jesus was crucified at Golgotha. What is the meaning of 'Golgotha'?

3. What part did Simon of Cyrene play in the events leading up to the crucifixion?

3. Describe three of the supernatural events that Matthew recorded when Jesus died.

4. What was Jesus saying when he cried out *"Eli, Eli, lema sabacthani"*?

5. What did the Roman soldier say after Jesus' death?

6. Why is the death of Jesus important for Christians?

7. If Jesus was a good man, and the 'Son of God' why was he put to death?

IN A GROUP

1. **Who was responsible for the Death of Jesus?**

   Traditionally the Jewish leaders have been blamed for the death of Jesus. The Gospels stress the part they played, even though the final decision was made by the Romans. Other people also played significant roles in the events leading up to Jesus' death.

   Look at the following list of people and write a sentence on the part they played in the death of Jesus:

The disciples	Pilate
Judas	The crowd
The Jewish leaders	Herod
Caiaphas	God
Jesus himself	

   Write a paragraph on who you think was most responsible for the death of Jesus.

2. **"Save yourself if you are God's Son."**

   Do you think Jesus should have avoided crucifixion? Discuss in small groups.

JESUS' RESURRECTION

LUKE 24:1-12

Early on the Sunday morning the women returned to the tomb to anoint the body. Mary Magdalene, Joanna and Mary the mother of James were among them (Luke 14:10). They were surprised to see that the stone which had been covering the entrance to Jesus' tomb had been rolled away. They were confused and went into the tomb and discovered that Jesus' body had gone.

They saw two men in dazzling clothes who asked the women: *"Why are you looking among the dead for one who is alive?"* (Luke 24:5). The men reminded them that Jesus had predicted his resurrection and told them that this had happened. In an excited state, the women ran to tell Jesus' disciples what had happened. The disciples did not believe them, but Peter wondered if it was really true and ran to the tomb to see for himself. He found the linen cloths that Jesus had been wrapped in but nothing more. He was amazed.

FOR YOUR FOLDER

1. What did the women see and experience when they returned to the tomb on the Sunday morning?

2. Explain the significance of Jesus' appearance to the women.

3. What would the resurrection have meant to the disciples?

IN A GROUP

"The importance of Jesus' death and Resurrection for Christians cannot be underestimated. The two events go hand in hand and are the basis of the Christian faith."

Look at the following reasons given and place them in order, starting with the reason that you think is most important:

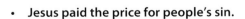

- Jesus' death and Resurrection shows that God can defeat the powers of evil, even death itself.

- Jesus' death and Resurrection prove that Jesus was who he claimed to be; the promised Messiah.

- Jesus' crucifixion changed the way people relate to God. The way is now open between people and God.

- The Resurrection shows that there is life after death This gives hope of everlasting life. Christians believe that they, too, will have life after death.

- Jesus paid the price for people's sin.

2. Do you think that Jesus' death is more important for Christians today than his Resurrection?

CLASS DEBATE: Did the Resurrection really happen?

"Belief in the physical Resurrection of Jesus is difficult in the twenty-first century."

- *Do you agree or disagree?*
- Give reasons for your answer.

Most Christians accept that the Resurrection of Jesus was a real event. However, there is an ongoing debate about whether or not the Resurrection really happened or if it was just a symbolic event. In groups discuss the following theories that have been put forward. See if you can fill in any information in the missing boxes.

ARGUMENTS AGAINST	ARGUMENTS FOR
Jesus did not die but was only unconscious. The coolness of the tomb helped him revive and he got out of it with the help of the disciples.	If this was true then what happened to Jesus?
Jesus did die but the disciples stole the body and then made up the story of the resurrection to convince people that Jesus was alive.	After the resurrection the disciples were prepared to risk everything for their faith. This is hard to believe if the resurrection had just been a trick.
Jesus did die but the followers of Jesus, in their distress, hallucinated because they wanted to believe that Jesus had risen.	The authorities were not able to produce the body to prove them wrong.
The women failed to see the body of Jesus at the tomb because they went to the wrong tomb.	

IN A GROUP

Discuss:

Does it matter whether the Resurrection of Jesus really happened or not?

Would it be enough for Jesus to live on through his teachings? Consider 1 Corinthians 15.12–19.

The Great Commission

MATTHEW 28:18–20

After his death and resurrection, Jesus appeared to the disciples in Galilee and told them:

"Go, then, to all peoples everywhere and make them my disciples: baptise them in the name of the Father, the Son, and the Holy Spirit, and teach them to obey everything I have commanded you. And I will be with you always, to the end of the age" (Matthew 28:19–20).

This is called **The Great Commission**. Down through the ages Jesus' followers have obeyed the commission, and today there are people in all parts of the world who believe that they too should carry out the Great Commission. Many Christians become missionaries and spread the Gospel throughout the world. Others simply follow the commission at home by living a life that is pleasing to God and points others to Jesus.

IN A GROUP

Some people think that it is fine to have religious faith as long as you keep it to yourself. Do you think Christians have the right to tell others about their faith? Give reasons for your answer, showing that you have considered more than one point of view.

FURTHER THINKING

How is the Great Commission carried out? Find out about the work of missionaries from your local churches and parishes or using the internet. Some examples include:

COCM Chinese Overseas Christian mission
www.cocm.org.uk

SIM Serving in Mission
www.sim.co.uk

CBM Christian Blind Mission
www.cbmuk.org.uk

Mission Africa
www.missionafrica.org.uk

OMF – Overseas Missionary Fellowship
www.omf.org.uk

FOR YOUR FOLDER

1. What is the Great Commission?

2. Name one thing Jesus commanded the disciples to do after his Resurrection.

3. How can Christians live out the Great Commission today?

Chapter 6

CHRISTIAN WORSHIP

THE DEVELOPMENT OF THE CHRISTIAN CHURCH

After the Ascension of Jesus, his followers obeyed the Great Commission by taking the Gospel to all nations. Many people became followers of Jesus' teaching throughout Europe and Asia, in spite of harsh **persecution** from religious and political groups that opposed the way of these 'Christians'. By AD380 Christianity was the official religion of the Roman Empire and it went on to spread across the world. Today, about one third of the world's population state their religion as Christian, and many different churches and groups meet to worship together.

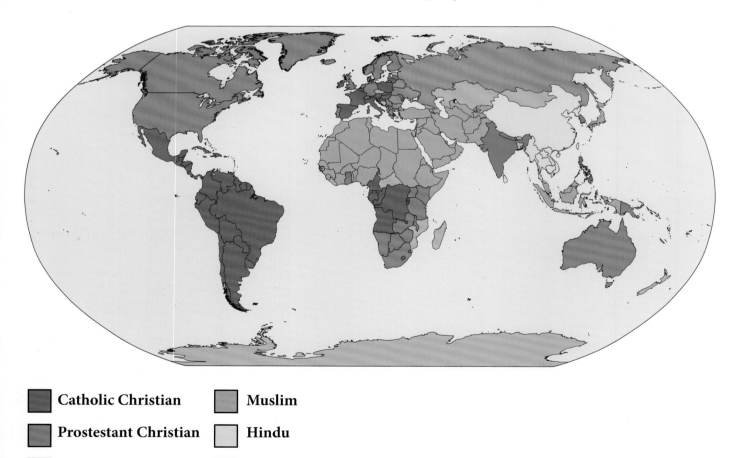

- **Catholic Christian**
- **Prostestant Christian**
- **Orthodox Christian**
- **Muslim**
- **Hindu**
- **Buddhist**
- **Other**

STYLES OF WORSHIP

Christian worship means showing adoration to God. Worship is not just about singing hymns of praise to God but can also involve prayer, movement and fellowship together. Some Christians would even regard their whole way of life as a form of worship.

No two Christian denominations are the same when it comes to how congregations worship God. Throughout Christian history there have been disagreements over the best way to express worship. Even within one denomination people may differ in how they prefer to worship.

Liturgical, structured worship

This style of worship follows a clear pattern at every worship service. It uses pre-written prayers and creeds, contained in special books or printed on leaflets. The term used for written prayers, creeds and instructions for worship is **liturgy**. Catholic and Church of Ireland churches are most likely to use this style of worship. In the Catholic Church they use the *Missal,* while the Church of Ireland use the *Book of Common Prayer*, or the more modern *Alternative Prayer Book*.

Other Christian denominations may not use a special book but their worship services are still very structured and follow a general routine. Examples include the Baptist Church and the Presbyterian Church. This means that the same order is used from one week to the next. Prayers tend not to be set and differ from one week to the next. This style of worship is orderly but there is also opportunity for variety.

Why do some people prefer liturgical worship?

- The idea of liturgy is based on the Bible. In the Old Testament the Israelites were commanded to recite special words when making offerings (Deuteronomy 26:3–15) and in the New Testament Jesus use the Lord's Prayer or 'Our Father' as an example of how to pray. This prayer is frequently used during liturgy in churches today.
- Some people feel that speaking to God should be done in a very respectful manner. The best way to do this is to use pre-written words.
- It is part of the tradition of the Church, to be passed down from one generation to the next.
- The congregation gets to play an active role in the worship service through reciting words and responding to prayers. They do not sit passively throughout the service; they have the opportunity to stand, sit, kneel, and go up to the front to receive communion.

Non-liturgical, spontaneous worship

There are two types of non-liturgical or spontaneous worship:

1. **Leaderless worship**
   Some Christian denominations, such as the Brethren or Quakers, choose not to have a minister or priest to lead their worship services. Instead anyone can contribute if they feel led to do so (although this does not apply to women in the Brethren Church). So someone might say a prayer, give a Bible reading or even preach a sermon without it having been planned in advance. This is spontaneous worship.

2. **Pentecostal or 'Charismatic'**
   This style of worship is lively and impulsive. Features include clapping, dancing and sometimes flag-waving, as well as singing.

   The word 'charismatic' comes from a Greek word, *charis*, which means 'gift', referring to the

gifts of the Holy Spirit (1 Corinthians 12:1–14). Three examples of gifts still in use today are:

- The gift of tongues – worshipping using a heavenly language
- The gift of prophecy –speaking God's words
- The gift of healing – helping to heal people with physical, emotional or mental illness

Why do some people prefer spontaneous worship?

- It is similar to the worship of the very early Church of the New Testament.
- Some believe that worship should be joyful, exciting and uplifting.
- Some people find following a liturgy boring or restrictive.
- It follows the example of worship given in the Psalms: *"Praise the Lord! Sing a new song to the Lord…Praise him with dancing; play drums and harps in praise of him"* (Psalm 149:1–3)

FOR YOUR FOLDER

1. Describe two different styles of worship.
2. Explain why some people might prefer each of these styles.
3. Which style of worship would you prefer and why?

THE TRADITION OF SINGING AND MUSIC

Singing songs of praise and worship to God has always been an important part of Christian worship. In some denominations everyone takes part in singing (for example, Presbyterian, Methodist and Church of Ireland); in others it may be the choir only that sings (for example, the Catholic Church).

There are various types of songs used in worship:

- **Traditional hymns**
  A hymn is a song of praise to God. Many churches have a strong tradition of singing hymns. For example, Charles Wesley, one of the founders of Methodism, wrote over 7,000 hymns, which are still used in different churches today.

- **Psalms**
  Psalms are songs of praise and worship found in the Old Testament. These have been put into verse form in a book called the *Psalter*. This makes them easy to set to music. Singing Psalms is popular in many Presbyterian churches.

- **Choruses**
  These are songs which use everyday language and mainly appeal to younger Christians. They often accompany hymn singing and are collected in books, for example, *Mission Praise*.

- **Contemporary Worship**
  In many churches, worship is led by a band. The music could include many different styles. New praise and worship songs are being written all the time.

There are various types of musical instrument used in worship services, depending upon the denomination:

- **Organ**
  This is a keyboard instrument and is one of the oldest musical instruments in western society. It uses wind moving through pipes of various materials to produce sounds which can vary widely in tone and volume. In many denominations singing is led by the organist, as well as the choir. Organs are a common feature in larger church buildings and cathedrals.

- **Choir**
  Many churches have a choir to lead the congregation in worship. As well as taking a lead in worship services, the choir can put on special events and normally work hard on their music for special occasions like Christmas and Easter. In a few Catholic churches there may be some very traditional choirs which sing in Latin.

- **Band**
  In some churches, worship is almost always led by a band. In other denominations instruments appear only on particular occasions such as **Folk Masses** in the Catholic Church. Church bands tend to be guitar-based, but can feature drums, violins, flutes, trumpets or any instrument. Some churches even count DJs and VJs as part of their worship team.

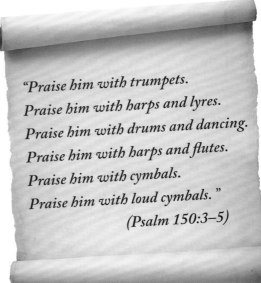

"Praise him with trumpets.
Praise him with harps and lyres.
Praise him with drums and dancing.
Praise him with harps and flutes.
Praise him with cymbals.
Praise him with loud cymbals."
(Psalm 150:3–5)

The Presbyterian Church recognises the importance of singing:

> "The singing of praise is another important part of Christian worship. Recognising that music should help to renew the mind rather than the emotions it is believed that music and songs must be related to the worship and the Word…We call upon our congregations to give a high priority to improving the standard of Church music, offering possibilities for wider training and experience to organists, choirs and others involved in congregational music. We call on all our people to put new heart into their singing and to let the inspiration and joy of Christian praise be heard in all our Churches."
>
> Coleraine Declaration 1990

IN A GROUP

1. "The playing of instruments other than the organ is disrespectful in church services." Do you agree or disagree? Give reasons for your answer.

2. Do you think certain styles of music exclude some people from participating in worship in a church service? Explain your answer.

DIFFERENT TYPES OF PRAYER AND THEIR PURPOSE IN CHRISTIAN WORSHIP

Prayer is a way of communicating with or talking to God. It is in itself an act of faith in God and Christians regard it as a means of deepening and developing their relationship with God. For most Christians prayer is seen as conversation with God, but for the purpose of worship services prayers are sometimes divided into categories, each with a different purpose.

Types of Prayer

- **Prayers of Adoration**
  In these prayers the person praying wishes to praise or worship God. For example, the Mass in the Catholic Church includes many of these types of prayer, such as the *Gloria* and the Eucharistic prayers. In the Protestant tradition the minister may use written prayers or compose their own prayers of adoration.

- **Prayers of Contrition and Confession**
  In these types of prayers people admit their own sinfulness and ask for God's forgiveness for that sin. In the Protestant churches they will form part of the normal worship service. In the Catholic Mass there are prayers of contrition in the **Penitential rite**, when the priest leads the people in the '**Lord have Mercy**' prayer or the '**I Confess**' is said. The **Act of Contrition** is another example of this kind of prayer, which may be said privately or when receiving the **Sacrament of Reconciliation**.

> I confess to almighty God,
> and to you, my brothers and sisters,
> that I have sinned through my own fault,
> in my thoughts and in my words,
> in what I have done, and in what I have failed to do;
> and I ask blessed Mary, ever virgin,
> all the angels and saints,
> and you, my brothers and sisters,
> to pray for me to the Lord our God.

- **Prayers of Petition**

  In these prayers the Christian usually asks God for things that they need. These may be physical or spiritual needs. Students often make prayers of petition when they are doing exams asking for the gift of wisdom, or the perseverance required to study hard. Those who are ill may ask for healing or the strength to bear their suffering. Prayers of petition should also express willingness to accept God's will, whatever the outcome.

- **Prayers of Thanksgiving**

  One formal example of a prayer of thanksgiving is the **Grace before meals.** In the Protestant churches prayers of thanksgiving may be said before the offering is collected. 'Eucharist' means 'thanksgiving' and in the Catholic Church the **Eucharistic Prayer** in the Mass is an example of a prayer of thanksgiving.

- **Prayers of Intercession**

  These are prayers for others, when the Christian prays on another's behalf. These prayers are most commonly said when someone is ill or experiencing a period of difficulty in their life.

  In the Protestant churches the minister may reflect upon a national disaster or a problem in the local community.

  In the Catholic Church, people may pray for a particular saint to **intercede** with God on someone's behalf. There is also a strong tradition of praying for those who have died. The **Prayers of the Faithful** in the Mass are an example of prayers of intercession, but often Christians privately say prayers of intercession for others.

" I feel closest to God, when I see my children play happily. I remember to give thanks. "

" I always turn to God when I am doing exams. It makes me feel calmer. "

FOR YOUR FOLDER

1. What do the statements above tell us about why Christians pray?

2. Which types of prayer do you think are being used by these people?

3. Copy and complete the table below. In the third column give examples of the kinds of words which may be used in each kind of prayer.

" I prayed a lot when my mum was ill last year. It helped me to deal with her illness and I felt I was doing something to help her. "

TYPE OF PRAYER	DEFINITION	EXAMPLE
Adoration		
Thanksgiving		
Confession		
Petition		
Intercession		

The 'Our Father' or The Lord's Prayer

Jesus taught this prayer to the first disciples, as a pattern for all prayer. The words of the prayer express some of the main beliefs of Christians. For these reasons it is seen as very important, and some denominations recite the prayer in most services. In the prayer we can see different types of prayer, such as praise, confession, thanksgiving, petition and intercession.

Our Father	When Jesus prays to God, he uses the word *abba* which means 'daddy'. This teaches Christians that God wants the best for his children and is as approachable as a loving father. God should be approached with respect, reverence and awe.
Hallowed be thy name	God's very name is honoured and holy. It should never be used in a casual way but is to be used in reverence and worship. This highlights the importance of putting God's glory first before personal needs are prayed for. The first section of the prayer is adoration.
Thy Kingdom Come, thy will be done, on earth as it is in heaven	The Bible teaches that when Jesus came to earth as a man, God's Kingdom also arrived. Through these words Jesus urges his followers to pray for God's will to be carried out on earth. The words "Thy will be done" help Christians to accept God's plan for them in life.
Give us this day our daily bread	"Bread", a basic food, represents all that a Christian may need. People do not just need physical food to be well. They also pray that their emotional and spiritual needs are met. These words imply that God will supply this help each day as it is needed. This is a prayer of petition.
Forgive us our trespasses as we forgive others who trespass against us	A prayer of confession. Jesus reminded his followers that only those who were prepared to forgive could ask for forgiveness. This is an important part of being a Christian.
And lead us not into temptation but deliver us from evil	This is a request that Jesus' followers will be able to resist any temptations that they may face. Christians express their faith that Jesus has overcome the power of evil by His death.
For thine is the Kingdom, the power and the glory, for ever and ever. Amen	*This statement appears in some Greek manuscripts of the gospel of Matthew, and is usually only said in the Protestant tradition.*

Hallowed be thy name,
Thy kingdom come,
Thy will be done on earth
as it is in heaven.
Give us this day our daily
bread

Using Technology for Prayer

The Vatican is endorsing new technology that brings the book of daily prayers used by priests straight onto iPhones. Father Paolo Padrini, an Italian priest developed an iPhone and iPod prayer application to be used for prayer.

The application includes the Breviary prayer book in many languages. Another section includes the prayers of the daily Mass, and a third contains various other prayers.
Monsignor Paul Tighe, secretary of the Vatican's Pontifical Council for Social Communications, praised the new application Monday, saying the Church "is learning to use the new technologies primarily as a tool or as a means of evangelising, as a way of being able to share its own message with the world."

Pope Benedict XVI, a classical music lover who was reportedly given an iPod in 2006, encourages methods of reaching out to young people through new media. During last summer's World Youth Day in Sydney, Australia, he sent out mobile phone text messages citing scripture to thousands of registered pilgrims – signed with the tagline "BXVI."

'Vatican approves iTunes prayer book', 17 December 2008, Telegraph, www.telegraph.co.uk, accessed 20 July 2009

FOR YOUR FOLDER

1. What are the benefits of using modern technology to spread the Christian faith?

2. Make a list of ways the Christian Church could use technology to spread the gospel.

Specific Prayers in the Catholic Tradition

The Catholic Church has some prayers that are unique to their worship:

The Rosary

The Rosary is a very traditional prayer of devotion to Mary in the Catholic Church. People recite set prayers including the **'Hail Mary'** while meditating on important events from the life of Jesus and his mother. Strings of **prayer beads** are used to count the repetitions of the prayers.

In the past the Rosary was a very helpful prayer for those who were poor and couldn't afford a Bible or for those who couldn't read. It helped them to learn important parts of the story of Jesus.

Mary has a very special position of honour in the Catholic Church as the Mother of God. The Catholic Church has many Feast days in honour of Mary:

8 December
The Immaculate Conception

1 January
Feast of Mary Mother of God

25 March
The Annunciation

31 May
The Visitation of the Blessed Virgin Mary

15 August
The Assumption of the Blessed Virgin Mary

15 September
Our Lady of Sorrows

Novenas

Novenas are a popular form of prayer in the Catholic Church.

- The name comes from the Latin *novem,* meaning 'nine'.

- Novenas are short prayers normally prayed over nine days.

- They are often ways of showing devotion to a particular saint and are prayed around the feast day or in a month dedicated to that saint.

- Novenas are often prayers of petition and request: For example, a novena to Saint Joseph, patron saint of fathers, to ask for the grace and strength to be a good parent; or a novena to Saint Anthony to find a lost article or possession.

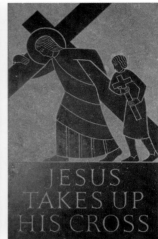

Stations of the Cross

The Stations of the Cross are a series of fourteen images, each representing an event in the last day of Jesus' life. They are a very important devotional exercise in the Catholic Church. People make their way from station to station, pausing at each to pray and to meditate on the suffering of Jesus.

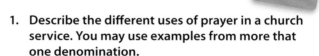

FOR YOUR FOLDER

1. Describe the different uses of prayer in a church service. You may use examples from more that one denomination.

2. Why do you think different types of prayer are used in church worship?

3. Explain why the 'Our Father' or Lord's Prayer is important to Christians.

4. Do you think the Stations of the Cross are a useful aid to prayer? Give reasons for your answer.

5. "Repetitive public prayers like the 'Our Father' or Lord's Prayer makes them become meaningless." Do you agree or disagree? Give reasons for your answer.

ORDERS OF SERVICE

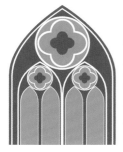

THE MASS IN THE CATHOLIC CHURCH

In the Catholic Church 'the Mass' is the name given to the celebration of the Eucharist. It is the central act of worship.

THE GREETING AND THE PENITENTIAL RITE

The priest welcomes the people and if appropriate says a few words about the theme of the Mass. For example, the Mass may be in honour of a particular saint or it may be a Mass for the sick. The **Penitential Rite** is important because the congregation acknowledge that they are sorry for their sins and ask God's forgiveness.

THE LITURGY OF THE WORD

This part of the Mass is made up of:

- **The Opening Prayer**

  If the Mass is being said on a Sunday or a feast day then the **Gloria** is said in worship, praise and thanks.

> **'Gloria'**
>
> Glory to God in the highest, and peace to His people on earth. Lord God heavenly King, almighty God and Father, we worship you, we give you thanks, we praise you for your glory. Lord Jesus Christ, only Son of the Father, Lord God, Lamb of God, you take away the sin of the world; have mercy on us; you are seated at the right hand of the Father; receive our prayer. For you alone are the Holy One, you alone are the Lord, you alone are the Most High, Jesus Christ, with the Holy Spirit, in the glory of God the Father. Amen.

- **Readings from the Bible**

  One is usually from the Old Testament and one from the New. These are usually read by members of the congregation (the laity). There is also a reading from the Gospel, which is read by the priest.

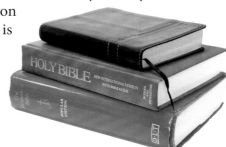

- **The Homily**
  Here the priest explains the meaning of the readings and helps the congregation to apply it to their everyday lives.

THE CREED AND PRAYERS OF THE FAITHFUL

A creed is a profession of faith said by everyone present. The Mass usually features the **Nicene Creed**. There are also around five **Prayers of the Faithful** or 'Bidding Prayers' in which the people pray for those in need in the Church, the world and the local community.

OFFERTORY

There is usually a procession in which the bread and wine are brought to the altar. Other gifts may be brought as well, such as money donated by the congregation. The priest says a prayer of blessing over the bread and wine and the people say:

> "May the Lord accept the sacrifice at your hands, for the praise and glory of his name, for our good, and the good of all his Church."

EUCHARISTIC PRAYERS

The Eucharistic Prayer is made up of the following:

The Preface or introduction, which includes a prayer of thanksgiving and ends with a prayer of praise and thanksgiving, sometimes called the *Sanctus*.

The Consecration of the bread and wine lie at the very heart of the Eucharistic Prayer. The priest repeats the words which Jesus used at the Last Supper: "This is my body… this is my blood" (Matthew 14:22–24). Catholics believe that the bread and wine then become the body and blood of Jesus.

The Proclamation of the Mystery of Faith follows the Consecration. All the people repeat or sing one of these responses:

"Christ has died, Christ is risen, Christ will come again.

"Dying you destroyed our death, rising you restored our life. Lord Jesus, come in glory.

"When we eat this bread and drink this cup, we proclaim your death, Lord Jesus, until you come in glory.

"Lord, by your cross and resurrection, you have set us free. You are the Saviour of the World."

The Memorial prayer which includes a prayer for the dead, a prayer for the needs of the Church, a prayer to honour the saints of the Church (perhaps the patron saint of that parish church) and a prayer asking for God's blessing on the Church.

The Concluding Doxology, which is a solemn prayer said or sung by the priest.

THE COMMUNION RITE

In this section, members recite the **'Our Father'** prayer and symbolically shake hands with one another as a **sign of peace**. The **Lamb of God** prayer emphasises the Catholic understanding of the death of Jesus as a sacrifice which takes away sin.

The priest then receives Communion and the people walk in procession to the Altar to receive the Eucharist. The Priest holds up the host to each person as they approach him and says the words **"The Body of Christ"** to which the person receiving replies **"Amen"**.

Did you know?

In the Catholic Church Eucharist bread, like a round wafer, is referred to as 'The Host'. Usually, the people only receive the bread at Mass, though sometimes both bread and wine are given.

CONCLUDING RITE

The priest says a final blessing over the people; **"Go in peace to love and serve the Lord".** The Mass usually ends with a hymn.

" When I go to Mass I feel it centres me and reminds me of who I am. I feel a sense of identity and belonging. I come away feeling strengthened and re-energised; ready to start a new week, mindful of what my real priorities in life are. For me there is something really spiritually nourishing about receiving the Body of Christ in Communion and the command to 'go out to love and serve the Lord' reminds me what the focus and purpose of my week at work and at home with my family should really be. "

CHURCH OF IRELAND ORDER OF SERVICE

Worship in the Church of Ireland follows the liturgical style – a set structure of words led by one person, but involving the whole congregation. The congregation follows the order of service in **The Book of Common Prayer** or another book.

Most Sunday mornings will feature a Service of Communion (always led by a minister) and a Service of Morning Prayer which can be led by a member of the congregation (a 'lay reader').

The order of service for the Morning Prayer service is outlined below:

Greeting, welcome and hymn of praise

The rector will welcome the congregation and invite them to worship God.

MINISTRY OF THE WORD

This includes:

- Readings from the Old and New Testaments. These readings follow the pattern set out in the **lectionary** – a book which states what passages of scripture should be read each week. A lectionary has a cycle of either two or three years so that the majority of the Bible is read over a period of time.

- Canticles. These are scripture passages set to music.

- All members of the congregation participate by reciting the **Apostles' Creed** – a statement of belief.

PRAYERS

Prayer forms an important part of the worship service. People pray standing, sitting or kneeling. *The Revised Catechism of the Church of Ireland* states:

> "Prayer is the uplifting of heart and mind to God. We adore him, we confess our sins and ask to be forgiven, we thank him, we pray for others and for ourselves, we listen to him and seek to know his will."

Written, liturgical prayers, such as the Lord's Prayer, are important in a Church of Ireland service.

There are three main types of prayer used:

1. Collects, which are short prayers with three parts.

Collects	
Addressing God	"O God, the author of peace and lover of concord, to know you is eternal life, and to serve you is perfect freedom;
A petition	"'Defend us in all assaults of our enemies, that we, surely trusting in your protection, may not fear the power of any adversaries;
Asking to be heard through Christ	"through Jesus Christ our Lord."

2. Prayers of **confession** (saying sorry for sin); prayers of **intercession** (praying for others); prayers of **thanksgiving** and prayers of **praise**.

3. Private prayer.

HYMNS

Hymns of praise are sung at intervals throughout the service. Depending on the congregation, these could be traditional hymns or modern worship songs, led by a band or the organist and choir.

SERMON

A talk based on the Bible readings. The minister explores the Bible text and its meaning for people's lives.

OFFERING

The congregation give offerings of money, collected in plates or bags. The money is dedicated to the work of God, as a symbol of each person dedicating their whole lives to God.

The money pays for the church building and for the various church organisations. Some is given to charities.

BENEDICTION

After a closing hymn the minister gives a word of blessing, such as "Go in peace to love and serve the Lord." The congregation then leave.

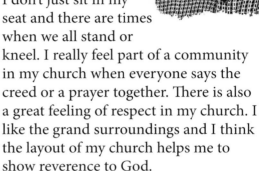

❝ I go to the Church of Ireland. I like that it follows a set liturgy because I know exactly what is going to happen next. I like that I don't just sit in my seat and there are times when we all stand or kneel. I really feel part of a community in my church when everyone says the creed or a prayer together. There is also a great feeling of respect in my church. I like the grand surroundings and I think the layout of my church helps me to show reverence to God. ❞

BAPTIST CHURCH ORDER OF SERVICE

Each individual Baptist congregation decides on its own format for worship services on Sunday morning, but most services follow an order similar to this:

Welcome and announcements

The pastor welcomes everyone to the service, particularly newcomers. Any announcements about events in the life of the church are made.

Prayer

Different types of prayer will be used throughout the service. This first prayer is likely to be a prayer of adoration, focusing the congregation on God. The service will also include prayers of intercession.

The pastor prays in his own words, and may invite a member of the congregation to lead prayer.

Hymns

Hymns of praise are sung at intervals throughout the service. Depending on the congregation, these could be traditional hymns or modern worship songs.

Children's talk

A talk for the children given by the pastor or another member of the congregation. Normally, children move to the front of the church and the speaker will talk to them face to face. This is sometimes followed by a children's song. After this, the children leave the main service and go to Sunday School or Children's church.

Bible readings

Parts of the Bible are read by members of the congregation. Many people follow the reading in their own Bibles.

The Bible is of central importance in a Baptist service. The Baptist confession of Faith states that:

> "The Holy Scripture is the only sufficient, certain and infallible rule of all saving knowledge, faith and obedience."

Sermon

A talk based on the Bible readings. The minister explores the Bible text and its meaning for people's lives. This will be the longest part of a Baptist service. Baptists believe they are listening to God through the readings and the words of the speaker.

Offering

The congregation give offerings of money, collected in plates or bags. The money is dedicated to the work of God, as a symbol of each person dedicating their whole lives to God.

The money pays for the church building and for the various church organisations. Some is given to charities.

Communion

After a time of quietness and reflection the Pastor invites those gathered to share in communion. Members of the congregation choose a song or hymn. There may also be a spontaneous prayer or Bible reading. The bread and wine are passed out to everyone in their seats. Everyone eats the bread at the same time, followed by the wine.

Benediction

The pastor gives a word of blessing, such as "Go in peace to love and serve the Lord." The congregation then leave.

" I go to my local Baptist Church every Sunday. The atmosphere is very relaxed and informal. My favourite part is the time of informal singing before communion where I sometimes get the chance to suggest one of my favourite choruses. Our pastor is a great preacher too and applies the Bible to everyday life. "

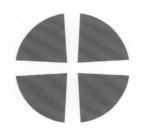

METHODIST CHURCH ORDER OF SERVICE

The style of Methodist worship services varies from congregation to congregation. Some will follow a structured liturgy from the Methodist Service Book, but most will vary their worship from one week to the next.

Most Methodist churches celebrate communion once a month, usually following a set liturgy.

Services generally follow an order similar to this:

PREPARATION

Call to worship

Usually with words from scripture, the minister invites the congregation to worship God.

Hymns

Hymns of praise are sung at intervals throughout the service. Depending on the congregation, these could be traditional hymns or modern worship songs. The Methodist Church has a rich tradition of hymns written by Charles Wesley, one of the Church's founders.

Prayers

The Methodist Catechism gives six different forms of prayer (adoration, confession, meditation, thanksgiving, intercession and petition), all of which may be used throughout the service. **The Lord's Prayer** may also be recited. Set, written prayers are not normally used.

At this point of the service there will usually be prayers of adoration and confession.

MINISTRY OF THE WORD

Hymn

Another hymn is sung to prepare the people to hear God's word.

Children's address

A talk for the children given by the minister or another member of the congregation. Normally, children move to the front of the church and the speaker will talk to them face to face. This is sometimes followed by a children's song. After this, the children leave the main service and go to Sunday School or Children's church.

Bible readings

Parts of the Bible are read by members of the congregation. Many people follow the reading in their own Bibles.

The Bible plays an important part in the worship of the Methodist Church, symbolised by an open Bible placed on the communion table.

> Some Methodists churches base their readings on a **lectionary** – a cycle of readings from Old and New Testament which ensure the whole Bible is read over the course of a year or more.

Sermon

A talk based on the Bible readings. The minister explores the Bible text and its meaning for people's lives.

RESPONSE

Prayers of meditation and thanksgiving

In some Methodist services there will be a time of quiet for the congregation to reflect on what they have heard. This is a chance to thank God for his message and for all that he has done.

Offering

The congregation give offerings of money, collected in plates or bags. The money is dedicated to the work of God, as a symbol of each person dedicating their whole lives to God.

The money pays for the church building and for the various church organisations. Some is given to charities.

Prayers of Intercession and Petition

The people pray for the needs of others and for themselves.

Hymn

A final hymn of praise to God.

The Grace

The congregation share words of blessing with one another:

> "The grace of the Lord Jesus Christ, the love of God, and the fellowship of the Holy Spirit be with you all" (2 Corinthians 13:13).

> ❝
> I love our Sunday morning service. Worshipping through music is very important to me.
> There is a big focus on community, and it's great to gather and worship God together. ❞

PRESBYTERIAN CHURCH: ORDER OF SERVICE

Presbyterian churches celebrate communion between two and six times a year, usually around special festivals.

The style of Presbyterian worship services varies from congregation to congregation. Most contain the same elements of praise, prayer readings and sermon outlined below:

APPROACH TO GOD

Call to worship

Usually with words from scripture, the minister invites the congregation to worship God.

Hymn or Psalm

Hymns of praise are sung at intervals throughout the service. Depending on the congregation, these could be traditional hymns or modern worship songs. The Presbyterian Church also has a tradition of singing psalms – songs found in the Old Testament which have been set to music.

Prayers of confession

Different types of prayer will be used throughout the service. Set, written prayers are not normally used.

This first prayer is likely to be a prayer of confession, asking God for forgiveness.

Children's address

A talk for the children given by the minister or another member of the congregation. Normally, children move to the front of the church and the speaker will talk to them face to face. This is sometimes followed by a children's song. After this, the children leave the main service and go to Sunday School or Children's church.

Hymn or Psalm

PROCLAMATION OF THE WORD

Bible readings

Parts of the Bible are read by members of the congregation. The Bible is central to Presbyterian worship. An open Bible is placed in the pulpit at the start of each service as a symbol that the congregation is now about to listen to the Word of God. There will be readings from the Old Testament and the New Testament.

Prayers of adoration and praise

These prayers give glory to God and prepare the congregation to hear the word of God.

Sermon

A talk based on the Bible readings. The minister explores the Bible text and its meaning for people's lives. This is the longest part of the service (between 20–30 minutes long).

RESPONSE TO THE WORD

Offering

The congregation give offerings of money, collected in plates or bags. The money is dedicated to the work of God, as a symbol of each person dedicating their whole lives to God.

The money pays for the church building and for the various church organisations. Some is given to charities.

Prayers of intercession

The minister leads people in prayer for the needs of others and for themselves.

Hymn or Psalm

A final song of praise is offered to God.

Blessing and dismissal

A word of blessing is given, such as "Go in peace to love and serve the Lord." The congregation then leave.

" Sunday worship gives me a chance to share in fellowship with others. I like the variety in the Presbyterian Church. It is both modern and traditional and appeals to all age groups. My favourite part is the sermon. I look forward to what the minister has to say. His sermons are really interesting and challenge me to focus on living out my Christian life. "

FOR YOUR FOLDER

1. Describe the normal Sunday act of worship in a denomination of your choice.

2. Why do most church services include a sermon or homily?

3. "Some churches place too much emphasis on preaching. This should not be the main focus of a service of worship." Do you agree or disagree? Give reasons for your answer.

4. Do you think it is a good idea to have the same order of service every Sunday?

5. "Church services are too long and too boring". How might you persuade a teenager who doesn't go to church that this is a false statement?

IN A GROUP

1. There has been an overall decline in the number of people attending church services in Northern Ireland. Why do you think this has happened?

2. Design an order of service that would appeal to your age group. Decide how long the service should be and what should be included.

THE IMPORTANCE OF THE BIBLE

The Bible is very important to Christians because it is believed to be the **inspired Word of God** and contains important teaching for believers. Jesus taught his followers that *"Man cannot live by bread alone but by every word that comes from the mouth of God"* (Mathew 4:4). So, many Christians see Bible teaching as 'spiritual food' because reading it helps them to grow strong in their faith.

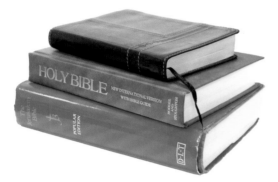

The Bible challenges Christians, helps them to develop, and encourages them to make a difference in the world and spread the Good News about Jesus.

How is the Bible used by the different denominations?

- In the Protestant denominations the Bible takes central stage. Worship services are based around the Bible. Leaders carefully select which part of the Bible is to be read and studied, and the sermon is based on those readings.

- In some denominations the sermon can last up to 40 minutes but is usually about 20 minutes long. Other parts of the services are also based on the Bible, for example, the reciting of the Lord's Prayer or the singing of Psalms.

- In the Catholic Church, while Bible readings are very important, the main focus is on the Eucharist. There are three Bible readings, one from the Old Testament, one from the Gospels, and one from the rest of the New Testament. A Psalm is also read during the Mass. The priest will give a homily – a short talk based on the readings, helping people to understand the implications for their lives.

- Some Christians like to meet with others to study the Bible. Usually, one person will prepare a topic and lead a discussion for those gathered.

" I used to find reading the Bible quite difficult until I found a translation of the Bible which I could understand easily. I try to read the Bible every night. I would often use a devotional book or reading notes. These guide you through a Bible book or a theme and are really helpful. "

" The Bible is God's word to me. If I want to know how God wants me to live, or what God is saying to me, I pray and read my Bible. Most times I read something that comforts me or encourages me. If I ever read anything I don't understand I always talk to a friend about it. "

THE IMPORTANCE OF PREACHING

Preaching is a central part of the worship service in some denominations, such as the Baptist Church, the Methodist Church and the Presbyterian Church. Christians believe that one of the ways that God communicates his word to Christians is through preaching. They see the Bible as the Word of God, and believe that the minister or pastor may be inspired by the Holy Spirit when preaching. The sermon is teaching based on the Bible, and it gives listeners a key to understanding and interpreting the Bible. Through the sermon Christians can learn how to apply Biblical teaching to their everyday lives. Bible readings throughout the service are based on the same theme as the sermon.

The minister or pastor will spend time during the week preparing for the sermon, through prayer and study. In some denominations the sermon will be the longest part of the service, lasting between 20 and 40 minutes.

In the Methodist Church both lay (ordinary members) and ordained (ministers) people can preach. In other denominations only the minister will preach, or there may be visiting ministers from another church invited to preach.

Sometimes a sermon will be aimed at those who are not Christians. People find themselves at church for all kinds of reasons, and the sermon is seen as an opportunity to explain the gospel to them. On other occasions the sermon might be to people who are already Christians, so the focus will be on developing and deepening their faith.

The importance attached to preaching is summed up in the words of the Presbyterian Church:

"Biblical preaching must be at the very heart of true worship. It must, of course, be presented attractively, and applied sharply to the actual situations and needs of our time."

The Coleraine Declaration, 1990

IN A GROUP

1. These are the views of some young people who attend Christian services every week. How would you respond to their views?

"I sometimes become bored at Mass. My attention wanders to the football match I will play in this afternoon. There's no point in me bothering to go if I'm too distracted to pray."

"There don't seem to be any young people involved in the service. I don't understand the words of some of the hymns and the sermon doesn't really relate to my life. Sometimes I think church is more for old people."

2. Copy and complete the table with some suggestions on what both church leaders and young people could do to make worship services a more meaningful experience. Some examples have been suggested.

Young people can	Church leaders can
Volunteer to take part in the service, for example, as a reader.	Keep sermons simple and shorter. Make them more relevant to younger people.

Chapter 7

CHURCH ARCHITECTURE AND FURNITURE

If you walk down the street you will pass many different kinds of buildings – houses, offices, businesses and shops. You may be able to guess from looking at them what goes on inside. Church buildings are often very noticeable, with eye-catching architecture or beautiful art displayed in their windows.

The design of most church buildings is loaded with symbolism, which means that you can tell a surprising amount about a group of Christians and their beliefs by looking at the building they meet in. The shape, style and size of the building, and even how the furniture is placed on the inside can reveal what is important to that church's members.

For example, if the communion table or altar is in the centre of the church building, then the act of Communion, Mass or Eucharist is probably central in the life of the congregation. If an open Bible, or the **pulpit** where the preacher stands, is in the centre of the church building then the focus of the congregation is probably on the Word of God.

CHURCH ARCHITECTURE

Throughout the UK and Ireland there are church buildings of different shapes and sizes. Even within the same Christian denomination there can be variety, depending on when a church was built, the location of the church and the beliefs of those who worship there. When we look at a church building we can usually work out what is important to its members.

FOR YOUR FOLDER

Think about the different church buildings that are in your town. Try to answer the following questions:

1. Describe the shape of the church buildings.

2. Where are the church buildings situated?

3. Are the buildings new or old? How can you tell?

4. What materials were used to build the church?

5. Do any of the buildings have a tower or a spire?

Church buildings are generally constructed in one of three shapes: the rectangular barn-style, cruciform shape and circular.

Some buildings may have other unique features such as a hall and tower, or be built in a particular way that was popular at the time, such as the Gothic style.

Barn-style

A barn-style church building is shaped like a rectangle. This shape is usually used by denominations that focus on the importance of the Word of God. It is associated with the Presbyterian Church and the Baptist Church. Attention is focused on the front of  the room, where the **pulpit** is normally placed in the centre. In some cases, where there is a larger congregation, there is a gallery at the back and sides.

Cruciform

The word 'cruciform' means 'cross-shaped'. Churches use the cruciform shape to highlight the importance of the death of Christ.

The cruciform shape is divided into the following sections:

- The **chancel** at the top of the cross contains the altar, the sanctuary and the choir.
- The **transepts** are the horizontals of the cross shape. They are often used as small chapels.
- The **nave** is the main part of the church where the congregation sits.

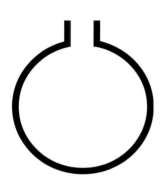

Circular

An increasing number of church buildings are being built in the modern, circular style. Wherever you sit you are able to look directly at other people. This communicates that the people are a Christian fellowship, participating in worship together, rather than simply being spectators. Every member of the church is of equal importance.

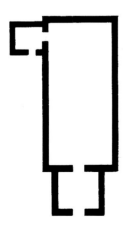

Hall and tower

This is quite similar to the barn-style, but has a tower attached to the rectangular hall. Historically, church buildings were places where people could shelter from attack, which is why some church buildings look more like fortresses. In more modern buildings the tower

is symbolic of taking refuge in God: *"The Lord is like a strong tower, where the righteous can go and be safe"* (Proverbs 18:10).

High towers decorated with steeples and spires pointing to the sky are a symbol for the resurrection. They also make church buildings a notable landmark.

Gothic Style

Gothic architecture originated in France and became popular in the Middle Ages and again in Victorian times.

The Gothic style is associated with high ceilings, pointed arches, large towers and spires. The design points to the mystery, holiness and majesty of God. It is a common style in great churches and cathedrals. The Catholic Cathedral in Armagh is an example of gothic style.

FOR YOUR FOLDER

Copy and complete the following table on the symbolism associated with church architecture:

Shape/Features	Symbolism
Barn-style	
Cruciform	
Circular	
Hall and Tower	
Gothic	

CHURCH FURNITURE

TEACHER'S NOTE

For this section you should study the architecture and furniture of a Catholic Church building and a church building belonging to one Protestant tradition: Church of Ireland, Baptist, Methodist or Presbyterian.

THE CATHOLIC CHURCH

Architecture

Catholic Church buildings can vary in style. Older buildings tend to be built in traditional shapes: cruciform; barn-style; hall and tower, normally made from stone and often in the Gothic style.

More recently some church buildings have been built with more contemporary designs, sometimes circular or oval in shape and generally more simplistic in layout. Many changes in the layout of the church were made as a result of Vatican II (the second Vatican Council).

Sanctuary

The word *sanctuary* means 'sacred' or 'set apart'. In the Catholic Church the sanctuary is an area at the front of the church building which contains the altar, tabernacle and ambo.

In cruciform buildings the sanctuary is situated at the east of the building, symbolizing the resurrection (the sun rises in the east and the city of Jerusalem, where Jesus died, is also in the east).

To access the sanctuary, the congregation moves from the main body, the nave, and climbs steps, symbolising drawing closer to God.

Did you know?

The second Vatican Council was a meeting of the Catholic Church's hierarchy (leaders), lasting from 11 October 1962 until 8 December 1965. It looked for ways to make the study of scripture and Church teachings more relevant to the current times. It also attempted to address the place of the Catholic Church in terms of the political, social and economic changes of that time.

FURTHER THINKING

How might the sanctuary be compared to the 'Holy of Holies' in the Jerusalem Temple at the time of Jesus?

Altar

The altar is the main focus of the building. It is a table, usually very ornate, made of wood or marble. The table will be draped in a cloth that matches the **liturgical colour** reflecting the seasons of the Church Calendar.

It is at this table that the priest says the words of the Mass service every day, and people come forward to receive the Eucharist. A chalice containing wine and sacred vessels containing bread (the host) are placed on the altar.

In the Old Testament an altar was a place where a sacrifice was offered, and the Eucharist is a reminder of Christ's sacrifice on the cross.

Catholics believe in **transubstantiation**, which means that the bread and wine become the body and blood of Christ. The congregation forms a queue in front of the altar where the priest gives them a wafer of bread (the body of Christ). Normally only the priest takes the wine (the blood of Christ).

Did you know?

In the past it was common for the altar to be against the front wall of the church which meant that the priest celebrated some parts of the Mass with his back to the congregation.

Since the second Vatican Council, however, a more open approach has been encouraged, with the altar in most churches having been moved closer to the congregation and the priest facing the people throughout the service.

In some churches this has led to the altar being in the centre of the church, creating a sense of fellowship, with the priest being among the people, rather than separate from them.

Tabernacle

The tabernacle is a special receptacle (box) which is situated behind the altar. After Mass the priest places the 'Blessed Sacrament' of bread in the tabernacle. This is a mark of respect for the presence of Christ in the bread. The bread may later be taken to church members who were unable to attend Mass because of illness.

The tabernacle is also a focus for those who enter the church during the day, perhaps to pray. When the consecrated bread is inside the tabernacle a red light, the sanctuary lamp, is lit to indicate the special presence of Christ. Catholics genuflect, ie bend their knee, in the direction of the tabernacle as a mark of respect to Christ's presence in the Eucharist inside the tabernacle.

The tabernacle in St Brigid's in Belfast has an image of a fish and a loaf of bread on the front. The fish was used as a symbol by early Christians to indicate their faith in Jesus Christ, Son of God, Saviour (the first letters of which in Greek make up the Greek word for fish). The bread represents the Eucharist.

At the time of Moses the tabernacle was literally a tent where the presence of God was said to dwell. Since then the word has come to mean any physical place where God is believed to be specially present, such as the bread and wine.

Ambo

The ambo is a reading desk usually situated to the left of the altar. Members of the congregation use the ambo to read the first two scriptural readings in the Mass, and the priest or deacon reads the Gospel and says the homily from the ambo. This is similar to the **pulpit** in other denominations.

Baptismal Font

The font is a container for the water used in baptism. Sometimes these are ornate pieces of furniture made from stone or wood, or simply a plain bowl that is brought into the church for baptismal services.

In traditionally shaped buildings the font is situated at the back, close to the main door, symbolising the first step taken towards God. In more modern buildings the font may be placed nearer to the altar.

> The Catholic Church performs infant baptism. Through the sacrament of baptism a Christian child belongs to Christ. However, an unbaptised person, who finds faith later in life, can also be baptised into the Catholic Church. Adult baptisms take place at Easter.
>
> Baptism is one of the three *sacraments of initiation* in the Catholic Church. Confirmation and Eucharist are the other two.

THE CHURCH OF IRELAND

Architecture

Most Church of Ireland buildings are built in the traditional cruciform shape. This emphasizes the importance of the cross to Christian beliefs. Some buildings are rectangular, but may appear to be cruciform inside.

Church of Ireland buildings traditionally feature high towers next to the main building. These often contain bells which are rung to call people to worship and to mark particular times of joy and sadness in the community.

Sanctuary

The word *sanctuary* means 'sacred' or 'set apart'. In the Church of Ireland the sanctuary is an area at the front of the church building which contains the Communion table.

In cruciform buildings the sanctuary is situated at the east of the building, symbolizing the resurrection (the sun rises in the east and the city of Jerusalem, where Jesus died, is also in the east).

To access the sanctuary, the congregation moves from the main body, the nave, and climbs steps, symbolising drawing closer to God.

Holy table or Communion table

The Communion table is the main focus of the building. It is usually very ornate, made of wood or marble. The table will be draped in a white linen cloth or one that matches the **liturgical colour** reflecting the seasons of the Church Calendar.

The bread and wine for communion are set on the table, covered with a white cloth. During the communion service the minister uncovers the bread and wine, and the congregation come forward and kneel around a low rail called the **communion rail**. The minister and others pass out the bread and wine.

> Not unlike the Catholic Church, the positioning of the Communion table has changed since the 1960s. Some churches have moved the communion table down into the main body of the church so that the whole congregation can gather around it as a family. This communicates that God is not distant and remote, but at the heart of the community.

Pulpit

The pulpit is a raised platform and reading desk in one, from which the sermon is given, usually by a minister or deacon. In the Church of Ireland, the pulpit tends to be positioned on the left (north) side of the front of the building.

The pulpit can be made from wood, granite or similar materials, sometimes elaborately carved with Christian symbols or an inscription such as 'Ye are ambassadors for Christ'. The pulpit is also decorated with a piece of fabric, called a **pulpit fall**. The pulpit fall changes to match the **liturgical colour** reflecting the seasons of the Church Calendar.

The pulpit is raised so that the congregation can both see and hear during the sermon, but in some churches the speaker chooses to leave the pulpit and speak from a lectern closer to the congregation, creating a sense of fellowship.

Lectern

The lectern is a reading desk used in the Church of Ireland for scripture readings. It is usually placed on the right (South) side in the sanctuary.

Traditionally, Church of Ireland lecterns are made of brass and shaped like an eagle perched on a globe – its wings outstretched to hold the open Bible. This arrangement is very symbolic.

- The strength and majesty of the eagle shows the importance and strength of the Word of God in the mission of the Church.
- The eagle is also a symbol of St John, the Gospel writer.
- The globe represents the world.
- The outstretched wings represent the Gospel being carried throughout the world.

Font

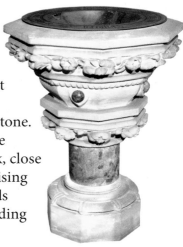

The font is a container for the water used in baptism. Traditionally these are large, permanent pieces of furniture, often made of ornately carved stone. In cruciform buildings the font is situated at the back, close to the main door, symbolising the first step taken towards God. This part of the building is called the **baptistery**.

Most Church of Ireland buildings now feature a portable font made of wood, with a steel bowl to hold the water. Baptisms take place at the front of the church, symbolising baptism into the community of the church.

THE BAPTIST CHURCH

Architecture

Most Baptist churches are quite plain buildings, simple in design, with a main hall, sometimes a secondary hall and a kitchen. Many are built in residential areas and are therefore designed to fit into the surrounding architecture.

Pulpit

The pulpit is a raised platform and reading desk in one, from which the sermon is given, usually by the pastor or an elder. The pulpit is the most prominent feature in Baptist Church buildings. It is usually made of wood, plainly designed, and positioned on a stage area at the front of the church. The physical centrality of the pulpit symbolises the centrality of the Word of God in the life of the church.

Communion table

This is a simple, wooden table where the bread and wine for communion are kept throughout the service. The table may have an inscription from the Bible, but its simplicity shows that worship does not have to be elaborate or complicated to please God.

It is usually placed in the centre, in front of the pulpit, symbolising that everything, including communion, comes from the Word of God. During the communion service, elders take the bread and wine to the people, who remain seated.

Lectern

The lectern is a reading desk used for scripture readings. It is a small, plain, wooden stand, placed below the pulpit. Some pastors prefer using the lectern instead of the pulpit for the sermon, as it brings them closer to the congregation.

Baptistery

The baptistery is a large, tiled tank, which holds the water for baptism. It is a very important feature in the Baptist Church.

The Baptist Church baptises people as adults by total immersion in water, so a large tank is required. Usually, the baptistery is directly below the communion table and is covered when not in use. There are steps leading down into the baptistery on each side for easy access.

THE METHODIST CHURCH

Architecture

Methodist buildings vary greatly in style and shape depending on when they were built. Often they are simple rectangular halls, but there are also more modern and more traditional designs. No two Methodist church buildings are the same.

The unusual architecture of Dundonald Methodist church.

Communion table

This is a table, usually made of wood, where the bread and wine for communion are set, covered with a white cloth. It is placed in the centre, at the front of the church building. Depending on the individual church the table could be plain or ornately carved or engraved with a phrase from scripture, such as: "Do this in remembrance of me".

During the communion service the minister uncovers the bread and wine, and the congregation come forward and kneel around a low rail called the **communion rail**. The minister and others pass out the bread and wine.

Pulpit

The pulpit is a raised platform and reading desk in one, from which the sermon is given, usually by the minister. The pulpit is usually made from wood and decorated with a piece of fabric called a **pulpit fall**. The pulpit fall can be plain or embroidered with a symbol, such as a dove.

In traditional Methodist buildings the pulpit is high up at the front of the church, behind the communion table. The physical centrality of the pulpit symbolises the centrality of the Word of God in the life of the church.

In more modern buildings, the pulpit is placed to one side, with the focus on the communion table, creating an atmosphere of sharing.

Lectern

The lectern is a reading desk used for scripture readings. It is usually made of plain wood, occasionally decorated with a cross. Some ministers prefer using the lectern instead of the pulpit for the sermon, as it brings them closer to the congregation.

Font

The font is a container for the water used in baptism. In most Methodist church buildings these are portable, carved wooden pieces with a steel bowl to hold the water. Baptisms take place at the front of the church, symbolising baptism into the community of the church.

THE PRESBYTERIAN CHURCH

Architecture

Most Presbyterian churches are built in the rectangular barn-style, often with a gallery. They are usually plain in design, showing that worship does not have to be elaborate or complicated to please God.

Pulpit

The pulpit is a raised platform and reading desk in one, from which the sermon is given, usually by the minister. The pulpit is the most prominent feature in Presbyterian buildings. It is traditionally high up at the front of the church, behind the communion table, emphasizing the authority of the Word of God.

The pulpit is usually made from wood and decorated with a piece of fabric called a **pulpit fall**. The pulpit fall is embroidered with the symbol of the Presbyterian Church – a 'burning bush' and the words *Arden Sed Virens*, which means 'burning but flourishing'. This reflects the Presbyterian belief that the Word of God will last forever.

In more modern buildings, the pulpit is placed to one side, with equal focus on the font and communion table.

Communion Table

This is a wooden table from which communion is served between two and six times every year. Depending on the individual church the table could be plain or ornately carved or engraved with a phrase from scripture, such as: "Do this in remembrance of me".

It is usually placed in the centre, in front of the pulpit, emphasising the Presbyterian belief that the act of communion takes second place to the word of God. During the communion service, elders take the bread and wine to the people, who remain seated.

Lectern

The lectern is a reading desk used for scripture readings. It is usually made of plain wood, occasionally decorated with a cross. Some ministers prefer using the lectern instead of the pulpit for the sermon, as it brings them closer to the congregation.

Font

The font is a container for the water used in baptism. In most Presbyterian church buildings these are portable, carved wooden pieces with a steel bowl to hold the water. Some churches have larger, permanent fonts and others have no font, simply placing a glass bowl on the communion table for baptism.

The font is placed at the front of the church, below the pulpit. This signifies that even baptism takes second place to the Word of God.

FOR YOUR FOLDER

1. Describe the location and function of the main furnishings in a church building of your choice. Some of the pieces you choose may include:

   • Lectern
   • Altar/communion table
   • Pulpit
   • Stations of the cross
   • Tabernacle
   • Font

2. Using relevant examples explain why there are sometimes differences in the architecture and layout of church buildings. For example, explain why some churches are plain inside while others are more decorative.

3. "Christians can worship God properly only in a church building." Do you agree or disagree? Give reasons for your answer.

4. "Ornate and decorative church buildings are a distraction for worshippers." Do you agree or disagree? Give reasons for your answer.

IN A GROUP

1. "Churches could make better use of their buildings to serve the whole community". Do you agree or disagree? Give reasons for your answer showing that you have considered different points of view.

2. "The content of worship rather than the place of worship is what really matters." Do you agree or disagree? Give reasons for your answer showing you have considered more than one point of view.

Chapter 8

CHURCH FESTIVALS

Throughout history people have marked the passing of the seasons with celebrations, rituals and times of feasting and fasting. You may look forward to Christmas and summer holidays as markers in your year. No matter what your background, you probably have annual traditions that you enjoy during the winter holiday. These traditions give a sense of rhythm to our lives, and allow us time to rest and reflect, to celebrate and enjoy ourselves.

Every religion marks significant episodes in the lives of key people. Most Christian festivals remember an important event in the life of Christ. Others may focus on the life of a special person, for example, Saints' Days. Whatever the festival, each is a time for Christians to reflect on their own personal faith.

Just as the school year begins in September, the Christian Church has its own 'Liturgical Calendar', which begins with the season of Advent at the end of November.

Festivals and holidays have almost always held a religious significance for people – literally 'Holy Days'. Before the birth and spread of Christianity in the western world, the year was marked by pagan festivals. For example, 25 December was originally associated with the pagan 'Birthday of the Sun', marking the beginning of longer hours of daylight. As Christianity spread pagan festivals were slowly replaced by Christian festivals.

The Seasons of the Church Year

Advent
Christmas
Epiphany
Lent
Easter
Pentecost
Season after Pentecost (Ordinary Time)

FOR YOUR FOLDER

1. Why might some people find following a calendar of the Church year a useful aid to worship?
2. Explain the purpose of celebrating Christian festivals.
3. Look at the table below, which outlines the Christian festivals that fall throughout the year. Copy out the table and describe how each festival is celebrated in a church in your area.

FESTIVAL	PURPOSE	HOW IS IT CELEBRATED?
Advent	To prepare for the coming of Christ	
Christmas	To celebrate the birth of Christ	
Epiphany	To remember the visit of the Magi	
Lent	A time to reflect and prepare for Easter	
Holy Week	To remember thelast week of the life of Christ	
Easter Sunday	To celebrate the Resurrection of Christ	
Ascension Sunday	To celebrate the Ascension of Christ	
Pentecost	To remember the coming of the Holy Spirit; the beginning of the Church	
Harvest	A day of thanksgiving for food	

IN A GROUP

You may already have noticed that some Christian festivals fall on the same date every year (for example, Christmas Day), whereas other festivals have a different date every year (for exmple, Easter Sunday). Can you think of a reason for this?

ADVENT

The word Advent comes from the Latin word *adventus* which means coming. The season of Advent is all about focusing on the coming of Jesus as Messiah and preparing for Christmas. It is a time of waiting and preparation, hope and joy. For many Christians it is a time for focusing on their own hopes, dreams and expectations. Some see Advent as an extension of Christmas, other churches, such as the Catholic Church, see Advent as an important season in itself.

Advent begins four Sundays before Christmas Day and lasts for the next four weeks until Christmas Eve.

How does the Church celebrate Advent?

Sunday Worship

Each Sunday of the Advent season is marked with special readings from the Bible focusing on the coming of the Messiah, a well as the second coming of Jesus.

> The Lord himself therefore will give you a sign. It is this: the maiden is with child and will soon give birth to a Son, whom she will call Immanuel
>
> (Isaiah 7:14)

Liturgical Colour

Different seasons in the Church calendar have different symbols, different traditions and even different colours. These colours will appear in furniture, decoration and clerical clothing.

The liturgical colour for Advent is purple. Purple is associated with penance – a time of reflection and turning away from sin. Purple is also associated with royalty, and Advent is a time of preparation for the coming of a king.

Rose pink is the colour for the third week of Advent, representing a move away from the solemn time of penance towards the joy and celebration of Christmas.

Advent Wreath

This custom originated in Germany. A circular wreath of evergreen represents the eternal life of God. It features four candles, symbolizing that Christ is the 'Light of the world'. One candle is lit on each Sunday of Advent. There are three purple candles and a fourth pink candle. Some wreaths feature a fifth, white candle at the centre, which is lit on Christmas day.

The Jesse Tree

The Jesse Tree is the family tree of Jesus, tracing his ancestry back to Jesse, the father of King David. It focuses Christians on the humanity of Jesus and reminds them of the importance of the Incarnation.

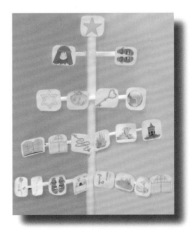

"The royal line of David is like a tree that has been cut down; but just as new branches sprout from a stump, so a new king will arise from among David's descendants" (Isaiah 11:1).

The Christingle

Some churches have a 'Christingle' service on the fourth Sunday of Advent. This is a carol service of Scandinavian origin at which every child receives an orange and candle wrapped in a red ribbon. The candle represents Jesus, the light of the world, and the ribbon stands for the blood of Christ and the love of God embracing the world.

The Advent Calendar

This is a twenty-four day calendar for the month of December. Children can open one window of the calendar each day to reveal a picture or a piece of chocolate. Some families may include a suggestion of a good deed that person can do for someone in their family or neighbourhood.

Advent Resolutions

Just as people make New Year's resolutions, Advent, the beginning of the Church Year, is a time of reflection when people reevaluate their lives. Many Christians decide on changes they want to make in their own lives and ask God to help them.

Did you know?

Like Lent, Advent is seen in the Catholic Church as a time for quiet and solemn reflection. Some traditionally joyous prayers, such as the 'Gloria' are left out of the Mass during this season. For these reasons, Advent has been called the 'little Lent'.

AN EXAMPLE OF ADVENT SERVICES IN THE CHURCH OF IRELAND

Sunday 7 December – The Second Sunday of Advent
10:00 am Holy Communion
11:00 am Sung Eucharist Communion Service

Sunday 14 December – The Third Sunday of Advent
10:00 am Holy Communion
11:00 am Choral Matins
3:15 pm Sung Eucharist Communion Service

Sunday 21 December – The Fourth Sunday of Advent
10:00 am Holy Communion
11:00 am Sung Eucharist
3:15 pm Festival of Nine Lessons and Carols

Sunday 28 December – The First Sunday of Christmas
10:00 am Holy Communion
11:00 am Said Eucharist
3:15 pm Evening Prayer

FOR YOUR FOLDER

Copy and complete the table below explaining how each Advent custom communicates the meaning of the season of Advent.

Advent Wreath	
Jesse Tree	
Advent calendar	
Advent resolution	

"
When I first think of Advent I think of how much I have to do and how many shopping days there are left . I have to get organised to take the children to see Santa and go to all the Christmas parties. I can start to feel quite stressed. Then I go to church and see the purple drapes, the beautiful Jesse tree which the Primary school children made and the Advent wreath on the altar and I feel a sense of peace and hope. **"**

Orla is 35 years old.

"
Because it is the beginning of the Church year I treat Advent as many people do New Year. It is time for me to make a fresh start. There is such a sense of joy and hope and positive expectation. So, I make my resolutions at this time and feel so much more positive that I can keep them and bring about real change for the better in my own life and in the lives of others. **"**

Julia is 65 years old.

"
We love Advent. It makes us feel happy and excited. Every day we open a window in the Advent Calendar. We get a little story from the Bible and a picture. Our mummy puts in a sweet as well. In school every Monday we light the candles on the Advent wreath. We can see we are getting closer and closer to Christmas and Jesus' birthday. **"**

Rónán is 8 and Éile is 5.

IN A GROUP

Read the statements above and summarise what each person understands about the importance of Advent.

CHRISTMAS

Christmas is the Christian festival that celebrates the birth of Christ. The word 'Christmas' is actually an abbreviation of two words: *'Christ's Mass'*. In our society Christmas is celebrated on 25 December. It is a national holiday and most places of work come to a standstill on Christmas Day.

The origins of Christmas

The story of the birth of Christ is told in two of the four Gospels: Matthew and Luke. Each Gospel adds something different to the story: Matthew mentions the visit of the magi – the wise men, whereas Luke includes the story of the shepherds, and the baby laid in a feeding trough.

Both accounts agree that Jesus' birth was miraculous, that he was conceived by the Holy Spirit and born in Bethlehem to Mary, who was engaged to be married to Joseph.

IN A GROUP

What comes to your mind when you hear the word 'Christmas'? In groups make a list of all the things you associate with Christmas.

Customs associated with Christmas

From November onwards, it is hard to forget that Christmas is on the way. Town centres are strewn with coloured fairy lights, Christmas trees and artificial snow on shop windows. Shopping centres stay open late and Christmas music seems to be played everywhere you go. By mid-December, most houses are decorated with Christmas trees, coloured lights and decorations.

Did you ever have your picture taken with Santa when you were younger? Why not bring your Santa photos into class?

With all the preparations complete, children go to bed early on Christmas Eve and wait for the morning. Some Christmas day traditions include exchanging and opening presents, Christmas dinner, pulling crackers, visiting family and friends, playing games and watching Christmas television.

FOR YOUR FOLDER

Do Christmas customs add to the true meaning of the Christmas story?

Look at the following list of customs associated with Christmas and find out their origins and what they mean.

In groups discuss each custom and decide if you think it adds to or takes away from the true meaning of Christmas – the story of the birth of Christ.

Christmas Custom	Meaning of custom	Does it add to the true meaning of Christmas?
Christmas cards		
Christmas tree		
Holly		
Mistletoe		
Carol singing		
Nativity play		
Nativity scene		
Santa		
25 December		

How is Christmas celebrated by the Christian Church?

Christmas is a very special time in the Church's calendar and there are many ways in which the festival is celebrated. Some denominations, especially those with a strong tradition of singing, hold carol services and children take part in Nativity plays retelling the story of Jesus' birth.

Christmas is also a time when people forget about issues that divide them and, often, different churches join together for special **ecumenical** services – that is, services that involve people of all denominations. In the Catholic Church and the Church of Ireland many people will attend a service late on Christmas Eve. In the Catholic Church this is referred to as the Midnight Mass, although in recent years it takes place as early as 10.30 pm. Such services can help people get into the right frame of mind for Christmas as often the day itself can be quite a hectic time.

Most churches hold a special service on Christmas morning. Carols, hymns and readings are selected and children bring new toys, making this an uplifting and joyful reminder of the wonderful gift of the birth of Christ. Many who would not normally attend Church join the Christmas day service to mark this special occasion.

In the Church of Ireland it is tradition for bishops to preach in their cathedrals, for example, the Archbishop of Armagh may preach in St Patrick's Cathedral on Christmas morning.

FOR YOUR FOLDER

Design a programme of events for a church over the Christmas holidays. Use the list to the right and your knowledge of what local churches do.

AN EXAMPLE OF CHRISTMAS CELEBRATIONS IN THE PRESBYTERIAN CHURCH

Sunday 21 December
11.30 am
You are very welcome to join us for the Children's Nativity Service. Tea and coffee will be served after this service.

Sunday 21 December
7.00 pm
A traditional Christmas celebration. Join us around the Church Christmas tree to sing carols old and new.

8.15 pm
Following the Carol Service is 'The Big Festive Quiz'. An evening of family fun.

Christmas Day
10.30 am
Come and join the celebration of the birth of Jesus. This short service will set you up to enjoy the real spirit of Christmas.

Focus on Giving

Christmas is a time of giving. Exchanging presents recalls the gifts given to Jesus by the magi in Matthew's Gospel. However, some people are critical of the focus on giving and receiving presents. People can feel pressured to spend a lot of money buying bigger and better presents. Some families can find it very difficult to balance their money after spending so much at Christmas. It is also said that spending so much money on ourselves is wrong, when there are so many people in the world without basic food, clothes or housing, especially when many Christmas presents are unwanted.

In recent years some people have opted out of the whole idea of giving gifts to each other, choosing to donate their money to charities instead. Some Christian denominations have provided people with alternatives:

The Church of Ireland

Black Santa

The 'Black Santa' tradition at Belfast Cathedral was started by Dean Sammy Crooks of the Church of Ireland in 1976. He was concerned at the money being spent on costly building programmes at the Cathedral. So he decided to stand in front of the Cathedral and beg for the poor and for charity.

Dean Crooks carried a small barrel in which donations could be placed, and dressed in the familiar black Anglican clerical cloak. Every day of the week before Christmas he 'sat out'. The local press described Dean Crooks as Belfast's Black Santa. He was succeeded by Dean Jack Shearer who involved members of the Cathedral Chapter in the Sit out. Under his leadership the event continued to develop so that by 2000, a total of £2.2 million pounds had been raised for charities over the previous 24 years.

All the money gathered is donated to local charities with a proportion given to Christian Aid. The range of charities includes medical research; those caring for children, youth and the elderly; the improvement of employment opportunities for young people and a host of small charities.

Most of the money donated is given by people who come to the Cathedral during the Sit out. Contributions are made by individuals, families, schools, offices and workplaces.
Some schools send the collection from their Christmas Carol Services or the proceeds of their Christmas Shows.

Source: www.belfastcathedral.org/black-santa

The Salvation Army

Christmas Family Appeal

The Christmas Family Appeal is a joint venture between The Salvation Army and the Society of St Vincent de Paul, supported by BBC Northern Ireland. The Appeal aims to make Christmas brighter for families facing severe financial hardship, by providing gifts to children at Christmas.

The Appeal collects and distributes donated Christmas toys and gifts for families in need across Northern Ireland. In 2008, toys and gifts were distributed to almost 5,000 families helping almost 12,500 children right across Northern Ireland.

Gifts can be donated at many outlets across Northern Ireland. Once donated, they are collected by representatives from the local Salvation Army or St Vincent de Paul who ensure they are passed on to local children in need.

Source: http://www1.salvationarmy.org.uk/uki/www_uki.nsf/vw-sublinks/5E2BFBD6D307EACD8025723000521DAD?openDocument

Donations in Lieu of Christmas Cards

Sending Christmas cards can be a tricky business. Who gets a card and who doesn't? Many people send cards to everyone they know for fear of offending anyone. Worse still, what happens when they are given a card last minute, and have nothing to give in return?

Some charities have developed a scheme to raise money for those in need by allowing people to give donations instead of sending Christmas cards. Families, businesses and town councils let people know that instead of sending Christmas cards, they have made a donation to charity. Likewise, people may ask friends, relatives and colleagues to make a donation instead of sending them a card.

82

The Methodist Church

'Better Than Bubble Bath – Extraordinary gifts for Christmas'

As many of us rack our brains for the perfect gift for that difficult relative, the Methodist Relief and Development Fund (MRDF) is encouraging people to do something life-changing this Christmas. It has launched an all-new range of gifts: ordinary-sounding things that make an extraordinary difference to people living in some of the world's poorest communities.

Extraordinary gifts provide a variety of opportunities, such as sending a child to school in Bangladesh or giving families in El Salvador a wood-saving stove. A colourful card and magnet explain all about the small miracle that each item enables – and with prices from £7 and gifts from around the world – it's not hard to find the perfect miracle – whomever you are buying for.

MRDF's Director of Supporter Relations, Amanda Norman, says: "Buying one of MRDF's Extraordinary gifts is money well spent – a meaningful gift that will change the lives of some of the world's poorest people."

Source: http://www.methodist.org.uk

IN A GROUP

Read the following accounts of what people think about Christmas and discuss the questions that follow.

Janine, 32
"Christmas is a time that I look forward to every year. I got married a few years ago and have two small children. They are getting to the stage where Santa means something to them so it is really exciting and reminds me of when I was young. It was a real pleasure buying them what they wanted, putting out a snack for Santa and his reindeer and seeing their little faces on Christmas morning. I can't wait until next year. We didn't go to church this year. We were too busy with the presents."

Adele, 15
"Christmas means being stuck at home all day with my family. I can't stand my brother, and Mum always ends up fighting with Granny. Granny always says something rude about the dinner and then it's a shouting match for the rest of the day. I can't even hear the TV. I end up going to my room and waiting for it to be over."

Sarah, 20
"I'm a student nurse and this year I had to work at Christmas. It was an amazing experience because I was on a children's ward. It really opened my eyes. Some of the little children were very sick and will not see next Christmas. I just thanked God for my health and my family. It was a wake-up call."

Tim, 23
"Christmas is a really special time in my church. Every Christmas Eve we all go carol singing around the town and give gifts to people. On Christmas morning all the children bring their toys to church. After the service the whole family gets together with cousins and aunts and uncles. This year we only gave each other a small gift and made a family donation to Action Cancer. My uncle died from cancer two years ago so it is important for us as a family to do this."

1. List the different ways that Christmas is important to people.
2. Is Christmas important to you? Give reasons for your answer.
3. Do you think most people understand Christmas as a religious holiday?
4. What do you think the Christian Church could do to make Christmas more meaningful to the average person?

EPIPHANY

In the Church Calendar, Christmas is a twelve-day feast which begins on 25 December and continues until 5 January. The new Church season begins on 6 January with the Feast of Epiphany. Christians associate this date with the visit of the magi, but it really marks three occasions when Jesus was revealed to be the Son of God:

1. **The visit of the Magi** (Matthew 2:1–12)
2. **The Baptism of Jesus** (Matthew 3:13–17; Mark 1:9–12; Luke 3:21–23)
3. **The Transfiguration** (Matthew 17:1–10; Mark 9:2–13; Luke 9:28–36)

The Greek word 'epiphany' literally means 'to show' or 'to reveal'.

During the following season, churches may focus on the significance of Jesus coming into the world and on his teaching ministry.

FOR YOUR FOLDER

1. What special name is given to the four weeks leading up to Christmas?
2. Describe the activities of the Church and individual Christians during this period.
3. Do you think that too much celebration during Advent takes away from the celebration of Christmas itself? Give reasons for your answer.
4. How can Christians remember the needy at Christmas?
5. What events are remembered at Epiphany?

THE EASTER CYCLE

Easter is the most important festival of the Church's calendar. *The Catechism of the Catholic Church* describes it as "not simply one feast among others, but the 'Feast of feasts'". Easter begins with Ash Wednesday and ends at Pentecost, lasting 90 days in total.

LENT

The first part of the Easter cycle is called 'Lent'. Lent is the period of 40 days (excluding Sundays) that begins on Ash Wednesday and ends on Easter Sunday. Lent is a reminder of the time Jesus spent in the wilderness, when he fasted for 40 days and nights, before beginning his ministry. It is considered to be a time of preparation for Easter and in the past many Christians would have fasted solemnly during Lent, giving up certain food, such as fish, eggs and milk.

Today there is probably a less strict approach to Lent. However, it is still a very important time in the Church calendar, with some denominations focusing on the importance of preparing for the celebration of Easter.

Shrove or Pancake Tuesday

Many of you will be familiar with the term 'Pancake Tuesday'. Supermarkets take the opportunity to advertise batter and lemon juice in the hope of boosting their profits. Families put their frying pans on to see who can flip their pancake the highest. There may even be pancakes sold in your school canteen on this day. But do you know the real meaning behind the day?

Within the Christian Church, Pancake Tuesday is called Shrove Tuesday. During the Middle Ages Christians would go to confession on this day, to be 'shriven'. This simply means that they received forgiveness for their sins.

As time went on Shrove Tuesday came to be remembered as the day before the long fast of Lent. It was necessary to use up all the forbidden ingredients such as fat and oil, and so the tradition of making pancakes arose.

In some parts of the world Shrove Tuesday has developed into a day of carnivals and parties. For example, in New Orleans, USA, there is a famous celebration called the *Mardi Gras* (which means 'Fat Tuesday' in French), which consists of parades, street festivals and parties.

Ash Wednesday

The first day of Lent is called Ash Wednesday. In the Middle Ages people wore sackcloth and covered their head in ashes as a sign of penance (being sorry for their sins). In the Catholic Church today people go to a special church service to be 'signed with ashes'. This means that the priest marks the sign of the cross on a person's forehead with ashes. The ash on the forehead shows everyone whom the person meets that they are sorry for their sins and intend to live a better life.

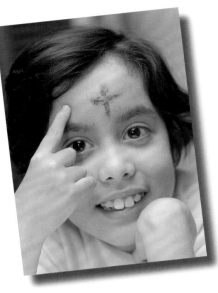

Lent in the Catholic Church

Ash Wednesday is an appropriate beginning to the season of Lent – a period of prayer and fasting in preparation for Easter. Giving to others who are less well off – 'almsgiving' – is another important aspect of Lent for Catholics.

Prayer

Lent is a period of prayer in the Catholic Church. Many Catholics make a commitment to go to Mass every day. For others it means making a point of finding more time each day to focus on God and on developing a relationship with him.

Fasting

This is a voluntary practice, and the extent to which people fast is a matter for the individual. It is a means of focusing on spiritual things rather than material things, and also helps to develop self-control.

Fasting means that Catholics limit the amount that they eat during Lent. For example, some restrict themselves to three meals a day, and so they say they are 'fasting between meals'. Catholics are asked by the Church to 'fast between meals' on Ash Wednesday and Good Friday.

Catholics may also **abstain** from certain foods. For some Catholics this means avoiding meat for all of Lent or, traditionally, on Wednesdays and Fridays.

Most Catholics choose to give up certain foods or hobbies that they find enjoyable as an act of self-sacrifice during Lent.

Today many Catholics practice fasting, not by giving up foods, but by giving up certain habits; for example, gossiping or criticising others or disobeying parents.

Fasting can also be an act of **solidarity** with those who do not have enough to eat.

Almsgiving

>
> Going without things does not consist only in giving what we do not need; sometimes it also consists in giving away what we do need.
>
> **Pope John Paul II**

Giving to others is an important part of Lent for Catholics. The Catholic charity Trócaire run an annual Lenten campaign which is supported by many people. Families collect Trócaire money boxes from their local church and return them at the end of Lent. Schools also get involved in fundraising.

TRÔCAIRE
Working for a Just World

"We work for a just world."

"We work with amazing people to bring about positive and lasting changes in some of the world's poorest places."

"Our programmes are carried out with partner organisations so local people drive the whole process and, in turn, their own development."

Source: http://www.trocaire.org/whatwedo

Amoo Gulyemina and her family live in Kilongo, Uganda, after being forced from their family home by conflict. They are pictured with the ox they recieved from Trócaire's Global Gift Plan. They also recieved seeds and agricultural training.

Amoo said:
"This gift will make our life easier. We will be able to grow more food and thanks to the ox, we will not have to dig the land by hand. This means we'll be able to plough a larger area and grow more food."

Trócaire 24 Hour Fast

For more than a decade, people have taken part in the Trócaire Fast – a fun and rewarding way to help raise vital funds for developing countries like Uganda. The idea is to stay off food for 24 hours as an act of solidarity with the world's poorest people, and collect sponsorship.

As well as the fast, Trócaire suggest a number of fundraising events including Cake Sales, Car Washing, Coffee Mornings and completing dares.

Source: https://www.trocaire.org/en/Donate

Lent in the Protestant denominations

There is less of a focus on Lent in some of the Protestant denominations than in the Catholic Church, but it is still an important time of reflection and preparation for Easter for many Christians. Some churches celebrate Shrove Tuesday with pancake suppers, and Ash Wednesday and Good Friday are fast days for Anglicans. The forty days of Lent may be marked with special Bible studies focusing on the Easter story or on Jesus' time in the wilderness. There may be special prayer meetings where people can pray together in small groups, or services where the whole church gathers for prayer and meditation.

An example from the Methodist Church: 'Buy Less Live More'

During Lent 2008 the British Methodist Church ran a 'Buy Less, Live More' campaign. Those who took part received an email every day of lent including prayers, readings and two challenges – one to 'Buy Less' (for example, 'Think twice about ordering that unnecessary trinket or gadget online'); one to 'Live More' (for example, 'Have a swapshop party – get your friends together to swap DVDs, books or clothes you don't want anymore'). A special Lent 'credit card' was produced to remind people to 'think before they spend'.

FOR YOUR FOLDER

1. What is the purpose of Lent?
2. Do you think Lent has any value for Christians today? Give reasons for your answer.
3. Explain the role of fasting, prayer and almsgiving (charity) in the season of Lent.
4. Why do Catholics receive ashes on Ash Wednesday?

IN A GROUP

1. Discuss the view that it is more valuable for Christians to take up good habits during Lent than to give things up.
2. Advent is a more important time than Lent. Do you agree or disagree? Give reasons for your answer

HOLY WEEK AND EASTER SUNDAY

Holy Week is the last week of Lent ending with Easter Sunday. During this week Christians remember the last events in the life of Christ, particularly his suffering and death. Each of the events in the last week of Jesus' life is remembered at some point during Holy Week.

PALM SUNDAY

The Sunday before Easter Sunday remembers the triumphal entry of Jesus into Jerusalem on a donkey. The people waved palm branches in honour of him and shouted 'hosanna'. Today **palm crosses** are given out in some churches.

HOLY THURSDAY OR MAUNDY THURSDAY

This remembers the events of the Last Supper Jesus had with his disciples before his death.

The word *maundy* means 'commandment'. At the last supper Jesus gave his disciples a new commandment "*to love one another*" (John 15:12), and gave a practical demonstration by taking the role of a servant, washing his disciple's feet. Every year the Pope carries out foot washing at a special service.
In England, the monarch used to wash the feet of the poor, but this has now been replaced by the giving of 'maundy money' to the elderly.

In the Catholic Church special services are held to bless the **anointing oils** that will be used for sacraments throughout the year.

After the Last Supper, Jesus prayed in the Garden of Gethsemane before he was arrested. Some churches hold all night prayer vigils in memory of this night.

GOOD FRIDAY

Good Friday remembers the day that Jesus died. It is a day of sadness and somber reflection on the death of Jesus. It is called 'Good' because of the Christian understanding of Jesus' death – a willing sacrifice that redeems the world to God. People have the chance to have their sins forgiven and to enter into the Kingdom of God.

Special services and prayer vigils are held. Many use the symbol of a candle being blown out to recall Jesus' death. Some Christians fast on Good Friday as a sign of sorrow.

HOLY SATURDAY

Jesus' body was taken down from the cross and buried in a tomb provided by Joseph of Arimathea. The Catholic Church holds an Easter vigil to prepare for the day ahead.

EASTER SUNDAY

Easter Sunday is the central festival of the Church year. It recalls Jesus' resurrection from the dead. Easter vigils that begin on Holy Saturday light Easter fires or 'Paschal candles' at midnight.
Dawn services are held at a variety of outdoor venues including seaside and hill top locations where people sing worship songs and watch the sun rise – an appropriate symbol of Christ's resurrection.

Regular Sunday services take on an air of celebration. Buildings are decorated with flowers, music may feature various instruments, and church bells are rung. Easter Sunday is also a traditional day for new Christians who have been undergoing training and instruction to be baptised.

FOR YOUR FOLDER

Use the information below to complete the table.

Teresa:
"I attend the Catholic Church and we have a number of ceremonies to celebrate Holy Week. Good Friday is a very solemn day and we don't celebrate Mass. All the statues in the church are covered. It is a day of mourning. We have a service at 3pm where we remember the Passion of Jesus by praying the Stations of the Cross. In the evening there is another solemn service. We all process to the altar and kiss the Cross. The Easter vigil on Saturday night is an amazing experience. The Mass really emphasises the theme of light overcoming darkness and we all light candles from one another in the darkness of the Church."

Graham:
"In St. Anne's Church of Ireland Cathedral there is a special service on Good Friday called the 'Service of the Three Hours'. It lasts from 12.00 pm until 3.00 pm and is made up of a series of 25-minute services of music, prayer, praise and readings, which highlight aspects of the crucifixion. People are free to come and go, which suits those who can only get a short break from work. It is a great chance for me to take time out of the rush of the day and to think about what Christ has done for me."

David:
"I am part of a Methodist Church and on Easter Sunday every year I get up early to celebrate Christ's resurrection at a dawn service. Sometimes an Easter fire is lit to keep everyone warm. We sing and pray together and read the Gospel accounts of the Resurrection. Often, we share communion together."

Tony:
"Easter is a very important time for my Baptist Church. We have communion on Palm Sunday in the evening, and on Maundy Thursday we have a joint service with a neighbouring Baptist Church. On Easter Sunday there is a big celebration service to remember the resurrection. Then on Easter Monday we meet in the afternoon in the Church grounds for a treasure hunt, which is followed by a barbecue."

Laura:
"On Good Friday my church meet with other congregations in the local area. Presbyterians, Methodists, Catholics, all praying and worshipping together. Events like these really bring people together and show the friendship and unity we share as followers of Jesus."

Holy Week in the Christian Church		
Day	**Why is it remembered?**	**How is it remembered?**
Palm Sunday		
Holy Thursday or Maundy Thursday		
Good Friday		
Holy Saturday		
Easter Sunday		

IN A GROUP

Read the following articles and discuss the questions below:

RELIGIOUS HOLIDAY TO BE AXED

By KAMEL ADMED, *Political Editor*

Schools are to be told to scrap Easter holidays and replace them with a non-religious 'spring break' as part of a fundamental overhaul of the way children are taught.

Despite objections from the Church of England and Christian pressure groups, supporters of the proposals say a specific Easter holiday is incompatible with a modern school system because it is on a different date each year. Moving to a fixed holiday would reduce teacher stress and pupil truancy and improve exam results.

The proposals say schools should be more ready to celebrate non-Christian festivals such as Diwali and the end of Ramadan. Head teachers will be allowed 10 'flexible days' each year to hold holidays which reflect the ethnic make-up of the school."

(*The Observer*, 27 May 2001. http://www.guardian.co.uk/uk/2001/may/27/schools.religion accessed 3 November 2009)

TRADITIONAL EASTER SCHOOL BREAK TO BE AXED

Hundreds of Mersey schools will... scrap the traditional Easter break. It is an attempt to make life easier for families who live, work and go to school across council boundaries.

The five participating authorities confirmed they will press ahead with the overhaul after winning support from the majority of parents, teachers and church officials.

Currently, term times can vary, making it difficult for teachers and parents to plan ahead because the two-week Easter holiday coincides with religious celebrations. Easter Sunday can fall anywhere between March 22 and April 25. But, under the unified model, Easter holidays will be replaced by a set 'spring break' during the first two weeks of April.

If Easter falls outside that time, schools will not open on Good Friday or Easter Monday. Schools will break up for summer towards the end of July until the end of August. The changes will be reviewed in 2011 to see how well they are working.

In Liverpool, 82% of people backed the alterations.

(*Taken from an original article by Ben Turner, Liverpool Daily Post, 30 July 2009 http://www.liverpooldailypost.co.uk/liverpool-news/regional-news/2009/07/30/merseyside-schools-to-synchronise-term-times-92534-24273128/ accessed 3 November 2009*)

1. Do you think churches can learn from each other's traditions regarding the celebration of festivals? Give reasons for your answer.

2. Do you think Easter should still be celebrated as a religious holiday in the twenty-first century? Explain your answer.

3. If Easter holidays in schools were replaced by a spring break, do you think it would make Easter seem less important? Make a list of arguments for and against this proposal.

SYMBOLS ASSOCIATED WITH EASTER

The Cross

Why would someone wear a symbol of execution around their neck?

The cross did not appear as a symbol for Christianity until the second century because it was seen as offensive. It was the worst form of torture and death imaginable, reserved for the lowest criminals and traitors. Roman citizens would not even mention crucifixion.

For centuries the cross has been worn as a simple expression of Christian faith. In the last hundred years it has become a popular item of jewellery and this has lead to some controversial discussion.

Some people object to the cross being worn as a fashion accessory: The death of Jesus is to be remembered with reverence, and the fact that the cross is sold as a trendy pendant in High Street stores is outrageous.

Other Christians argue that the Jesus is central to our culture, and the development of the cross into a fashion item shows that there is a deep, spiritual longing to connect with something meaningful. In a world of worries, change and fractured lives, the cross points to something deep and unchanging.

IN A GROUP

"A cross or crucifix should only be worn by people who appreciate its true meaning". Do you agree or disagree? Discuss your reasons.

Light

Light is a very important symbol for Christians. Jesus said "I am the Light of the World" (John 8:12), and taught his followers to shine like lights (Matthew 5:14). Some Good Friday services end with the blowing out of a single candle – a powerful symbol of Christ's death.

In the Catholic Easter Vigil Mass there is a solemn procession through a darkened Church carrying the **Paschal** candle. Each member of the congregation lights a smaller candle from the Paschal Candle or from each other, symbolising the light of Christ being passed on. The light symbolises:

- **Life** – Jesus' Resurrection brings new Life because he overcame death which is symbolised by darkness.
- **Knowledge** – Lack of knowledge is sometimes described as darkness of mind. The mind which is full of knowledge and wisdom is said to be 'enlightened'.

New Life

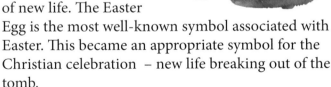

These symbols all have pre-Christian roots. Spring was celebrated as the coming forth of new life. The Easter Egg is the most well-known symbol associated with Easter. This became an appropriate symbol for the Christian celebration – new life breaking out of the tomb.

FOR YOUR FOLDER

1. What event is remembered on Good Friday?

2. Do you think that Easter should have a fixed annual date just like Christmas? Explain your answer.

3. Describe how Easter is celebrated in the Christian Church.

4. "Christmas is a more important festival than Easter." Do you agree or disagree?

PENTECOST

Pentecost is a celebration of the coming of the Holy Spirit which was promised by Jesus (John 14:16). The Holy Spirit gave the followers of Jesus power to go out and spread the gospel, as Jesus had commanded them to do. Over three thousand people were converted to Christianity on the Day of Pentecost, so it is sometimes celebrated as the 'birthday' of the Church. Pentecost falls fifty days after Easter.

In some churches Pentecost is called 'Whitsun'. It was a tradition that baptisms would be carried out at this time of year, which meant the church would be full of newly baptised people wearing white robes. It became known as 'White Sunday', and then 'Whitsun'.

In some churches the Day of Pentecost is also a time to thank God for the gifts of the Holy Spirit. Symbolism such as flames of fire or a white dove could be displayed on church walls at Pentecost. These symbols remind believers about the power of God and the peace that the Holy Spirit brings.

FOR YOUR FOLDER

1. Explain why Pentecost is important to Christians.
2. "Pentecost is as important for Christians as Christmas or Easter. It should be a public holiday." Do you agree or disagree? Give reasons, showing that you have considered more than one point of view.

SAINT'S DAYS

Saints days are celebrated in the Church of Ireland and the Catholic Church. In the early Church the term 'saint' referred to follower of Jesus. As the church grew and developed 'saint' came to mean those who lived a life of exemplary holiness and devotion to God. They showed they were close to God by the choices they made and the way they lived their life. Some served others in a selfless way; others brought people to the faith by their preaching, teaching and example. Some were even prepared to die for their faith. They are called **Martyrs.**

FURTHER THINKING

Saint Stephen was the first Christian martyr. What can you find out about Saint Stephen's day?

All Saint's Day

This celebration on 1 November was originally instituted to honour all the Christian martyrs, but has extended to remembering all the Christian saints. It is a holy day of Obligation in the Catholic Church, which means Catholics should mark the day by attending Mass.

Patron Saints

It became common practice in the Catholic Church to seek the prayers of saints for certain things. Gradually, certain saints came to be seen as guardians of a place, trade or group. Often, this would relate to the things the saint was interested in during their lifetime. For example, Saint Joseph became the patron saint of carpenters. Some saints who suffered particular illnesses, or cared for those who did, became patron saints for that disease or illness.

Why celebrate saints' days?

- Some Christians believe that it is important to celebrate saints' days to **remember** the great men and women of the Church. They have done great things for the Church and their achievements are celebrated with a special day in their honour.

- Saints are also an **inspiration** to other Christians. They are good examples of commitment to the faith and love and service of God and neighbour.

- The Catholic Church believes that saints are already in heaven and are especially close to God. This means that Christians can ask the saint to pray on their behalf. This is viewed similarly to asking a friend to pray for you.

Relics

The Catholic Church especially are interested in the relics of the saint. Anything that was associated with them in life, be it their clothes, objects they have had contact with, or their bones are seen as important and holy. They are preserved and protected and are sometimes objects of devotion.

The chains of St. Peter are kept in Rome.

FOR YOUR FOLDER

1. What is a saint?
2. Explain the role of saints in the Catholic Church.
3. What is a Patron saint?

HARVEST

The Harvest festival is mainly celebrated in Protestant churches. It is a time to thank God for the food we eat, and for all that God provides. Harvest Thanksgiving Services take place in the autumn and, in the past, would have been associated with farmers bringing in their crops to supply the local community with enough food to last the year.

Church buildings are decorated with flowers, fruit and vegetables. There may be a table for people to bring gifts of food, which will later be distributed to the poor, or elderly people stuck at home. Bible readings and hymns will be carefully chosen to reflect the theme of God's provision. The service is also a chance for Christians to be reminded of those who do not have enough 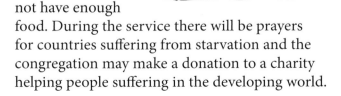 food. During the service there will be prayers for countries suffering from starvation and the congregation may make a donation to a charity helping people suffering in the developing world.

The Container Ministry

One example of an organisation working to provide appropriate resources to developing countries is the Container Ministry. Based in Lurgan, Co Armagh, the Container Ministry is part of the Methodist Missionary Society (Ireland).

People donate items such as computers, tools, educational resources and hospital equipment which volunteers assess and load into container lorries which are shipped across the world. This is in response to specific requests from overseas partner churches.

FOR YOUR FOLDER

1. Explain what different churches do to thank God for the harvest.
2. Do you think harvest thanksgiving services have any relevance today?

IN A GROUP

"The Church today spends too much time focusing on past events and not enough on meeting the needs of people living in the twenty-first century."

Do you agree or disagree? Give reasons for your answer showing you have considered different points of view.

A Prayer for the Container Ministry

Thank you, God, that we live in a prosperous land with a temperate climate.

Forgive us when we take for granted your blessings, waste your gifts, dump good food, and are poor stewards of valuable resources.

Thank you for the work of the Container Ministry …
We ask for your continued provision for the Container ministry to re-cycle and provide new products in the service of the world Church.

Give safe passage by land and sea and through customs at point of entry.

Guide this ministry as it changes to meet the changing needs of the world.

We offer this prayer in the name of our Lord Jesus Christ who fed the hungry, blessed the children, healed the sick and preached the good news to the poor.

Amen

Source: http://www.irishmethodist.org/mmsi/container.htm

Chapter 9

SACRAMENTS AND ORDINANCES

A sacrament is a formal religious ceremony which St Augustine described as "A visible sign of an invisible reality". Taking part in ceremonies like Baptism or Communion enables people to focus on God and experience God in a particular way. The Presbyterian, Methodist, Church of Ireland and Catholic churches all accept that God's grace is given in a special way to a person when they receive a sacrament.

The Baptist Church does not believe that any special grace is given through these ceremonies. They are seen as simply symbolic. The Baptist Church does not use the word 'sacrament', but refers to Baptism and Communion as **ordinances** because they were instituted and ordained by Jesus.

Most Protestant denominations recognise baptism and communion as sacraments or ordinances. The Quakers and the Salvation Army have no sacraments or ordinances. The Catholic Church recognises seven sacraments: Baptism; Confirmation; Eucharist; Reconciliation (confession); Anointing of the sick; Marriage and Holy Orders (becoming a Priest).

This chapter will look at Catholic and Protestant approaches to Baptism and Eucharist (Communion).

BAPTISM

Baptism is a symbolic washing in water that is often seen as a ceremony of initiation into the Church. Jesus himself was baptised (see chapter 2), and in the Great Commission orders his followers: *"Go, then, to all peoples everywhere and make them my disciples: baptise them in the name of the Father, the Son, and the Holy Spirit"* (Matthew 28:19).

Churches differ on whether people should be baptised as infants or as adults, and on what exactly the symbolism of Baptism means.

TEACHER'S NOTE

For this section you should study the practice of Baptism in the Catholic Church and one Protestant tradition: Church of Ireland, Baptist, Methodist or Presbyterian.

(Continue reading from page 105.)

BAPTISM IN THE CATHOLIC CHURCH

There are three main points about baptism in the Catholic Church. These will be considered in more detail in the following section:

1. Baptism is a sacrament.
2. It is for the infants of members of the Catholic Church, or adults who have not been baptised.
3. It is carried out by pouring water over the head three times.

Who is baptised?

The Catholic Church baptises infants as a sign of becoming part of God's family, the Church. This usually happens in the first few weeks of the child's life. Sometimes adults who have not already been baptised can receive the sacrament.

The Role of Godparents

In the Catholic Church, people, usually family friends, are chosen to be godparents. They are representative of the Christian family and agree to support the parents in bringing the child up in the faith. During the ceremony the priest will ask the godparents whether they are prepared to help the parents in this way. For this reason the Catholic Church asks that one of the godparents is a Catholic themselves.

Ceremony of Baptism in the Catholic Church

Baptisms usually take place every week. There may be just one family presenting a child, or a few baptisms at the same time. The Easter service will sometimes include baptism. People invite family and friends to join them at the ceremony.

The baptism ceremony can be divided into four parts:

1. At the Door

The ceremony of baptism begins at the door of the Church. This is symbolic of the child's entrance into the Christian Community. Here the priest will ask the name which is to be given to the infant and outline the responsibility of the parents and the godparents. He will say:

> *"You have asked to have your child baptised. In doing so you are accepting the responsibility of training him in the practice of the faith. It will be your duty to bring him up according to God's Commandments as Christ taught us by loving God and our neighbour…"*

The priest will then ask the godparents if they are willing to help the parents in this task. Then the child is welcomed into the Christian family with the words,

> *"(Name), the Christian community welcomes you with great joy. In its name I claim you for Christ our Saviour by the sign of his cross. I now trace the sign of the Cross on your forehead and invite your parents and godparents to do the same."*

2. At the Book

The next stage of the ceremony takes place at the Book. Scripture readings usually include the story of the baptism of Jesus or his conversation with Nicodemus (John 3:1–21). There will be a short explanation of the readings after which there will be **'Prayers of the Faithful'** for the child, parents and godparents. The child is then anointed on the chest with the **Oil of Catechumens** sometimes called the **Oil of Salvation.**

> *"We anoint you with the oil of Salvation in the name of Christ our Saviour: may he strengthen you with his power…"*

3. At the Font

The priest blesses the water with which the baby will be baptised. The parents and the godparents are asked to renew their own faith promises – another reminder of their responsibility to bring the child up in the faith.

> *"Dear parents and Godparents… On your part you must make it your constant care to bring him/her up in the practise of the faith…"*

The baptismal promises are made on behalf of the child in the form of question and answer:

> *"Do you reject Satan and all his works and all his empty promises?*
>
> *"Do you believe in God the Father Almighty, creator of heaven and earth?*
>
> *"Do you believe in Jesus Christ, his only son our Lord, who was born of the Virgin Mary, was crucified, died and was buried, rose from the dead and is now seated at the right hand of the Father?"*

The parents reply **"***We Do.***"**

The water is poured three times over the forehead of the baby with the words:

> *"(Name), I baptise you in the name of the Father and of the Son and of the Holy Spirit"*

The child is then anointed with the **Oil of Chrism**. The baptismal candle is lit by one of the parents from the paschal candle (which represents Jesus' Resurrection). The priest says:

> *"Receive the light of Christ… to be kept burning brightly… this child of yours is to walk always as a child of the light. May he/she keep the flame of faith alive in his/her heart."*

4. At the Altar

The child and their family look forward to the Eucharist, the second **sacrament of Initiation** into the Church. Everyone says the **'Our Father'** and prayers are offered for the mother and father and for all those who have attended the baptism.

The priest touches the baby's ears and mouth and prays that they may receive God's word and proclaim the faith.

BELIEFS ABOUT BAPTISM

Baptism is one of the seven sacraments of the Catholic Church. It is the first of the sacraments of initiation which will make the person a full member of the Church.

These sacraments of initiation are **Baptism, Eucharist and Confirmation.** Baptism is usually administered by a priest but any Catholic can carry out baptism. This may be necessary in an emergency, if someone becomes ill.

Catholics believe that:
- In the sacrament of Baptism the child first meets the risen Jesus
- The child begins a new life in Christ
- The child receives the grace of God
- The child becomes a member of the Church
- The child is cleansed of Original sin
- The child first receives the Holy Spirit but will receive the fullness of the Spirit at Confirmation

> The Sacraments of initiation, Baptism, Confirmation and the Eucharist lay the foundations of every Christian life… The faithful are born anew by baptism, strengthened by the sacrament of Confirmation, and receive in the Eucharist the food of eternal life.
>
> *Catechism of the Catholic Church (1212)*

SYMBOLISM OF BAPTISM

1. Water

Water is the central symbol of baptism. The Catholic Church teaches that human beings are born sinful (original sin), so Baptism is seen as washing away the stain of sin.

Water is also a powerful symbol in the Old Testament:

- In the Creation story in Genesis 1:1–10 it is a source of **power** and **strength;**
- in the story of Noah, God sent the flood in punishment for man's sins, so it can be a symbol of **death**
- in Exodus 14:15–31 it sets people **free** from slavery and so is a sign of **hope** and **new beginnings**

In Catholic Baptism, water signifies **death to the old, sinful self**, **freedom from the power of evil** and **new life in Christ**.

2. Anointing Oils

The **oil of salvation** symbolises that the child is given the strength to fight against evil and to do good. The oil of **chrism** is used to show that the child has now been given the task **of carrying out the work of Christ**, just as people in the Old Testament were anointed for special tasks.

3. Paschal Candle

The Paschal Candle represents Christ overcoming death and sin in the same way as light overcomes darkness.

4. White Garment

In Catholic baptism the baby is always clothed in a white garment. In baptism they have *"become clothed in Christ"* (Galatians 3:27). It is a sign of happiness, new life, innocence and sinlessness.

5. Name

The chosen name of the child is sometimes a saint's name. The child can try to live up to the qualities of that saint.

6. The sign of the Cross

The sign of the cross traced on the child's forehead is a symbol of ownership – the child now belongs to God the Father.

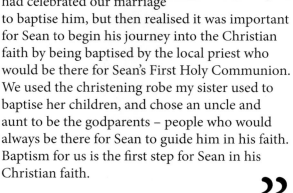

" Before Sean was even born, my husband and I began to discuss his baptism. For us, it was a very important family and religious occasion. We had thought about asking a priest who had celebrated our marriage to baptise him, but then realised it was important for Sean to begin his journey into the Christian faith by being baptised by the local priest who would be there for Sean's First Holy Communion. We used the christening robe my sister used to baptise her children, and chose an uncle and aunt to be the godparents – people who would always be there for Sean to guide him in his faith. Baptism for us is the first step for Sean in his Christian faith. **"**

BAPTISM IN THE CHURCH OF IRELAND

BAPTISM IN THE CHURCH OF IRELAND

There are three main points about baptism in the Church of Ireland. These will be considered in more detail in the following section:

1. Baptism is a sacrament.
2. It is for the infants of believers or for adults who were not baptised as infants.
3. It is carried out by pouring water three times over the person's head.

Who is baptised?

The Church of Ireland usually baptises infants, normally in the first few weeks of the child's life as a sign of acceptance into the family of the Church. Sometimes adults who have not already been baptised can receive the sacrament.

The Role of Godparents

Usually, family friends are chosen to be godparents, also known as sponsors. During the ceremony they promise to support the parents in bringing the child up in the faith. It is considered a privilege and a responsibility.

A CEREMONY OF BAPTISM IN THE CHURCH OF IRELAND

Most baptisms are carried out in public in front of the local congregation as the ceremony is a sign of welcoming the child into the family of the church. The sacrament of baptism takes place after the ministry of the word.

At the baptism the parents and godparents are required to make promises on behalf of the child and to undertake to "encourage them in the life and faith of the Christian Community" and to "care for them, and help them to take their place within the life and worship of Christ's Church" (*Book of Common Prayer*, page 361).

The parents and the godparents are asked three questions:

- Do you turn to Christ?
- Do you renounce the Devil and all his works?
- Will you obey and serve Christ?

The water is blessed at the font. The parents are asked to affirm the Apostles' Creed. The minister then holds the infant, pours water over its head three times, while saying the words:

"(Name), I baptise you in the Name of the Father and of the Son and of the Holy Spirit."

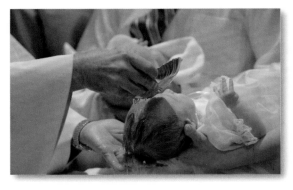

The minister makes the sign of the cross on the infant's forehead.

As baptism is the beginning of the Christian life, a lighted candle may be presented with the words "You have received the light of Christ; walk in this light all the days of your life. Shine as a light in the world to the glory of God the Father" (*Book of Common Prayer*, page 367).

The congregation welcomes the infant into the church with the words:

> "*God has adopted you by baptism into his church. We therefore receive you into the household of faith, as a member of the body of Christ, as the child of the same heavenly Father, and as an inheritor with us of the kingdom of God.*"

Everyone recites the Lord's Prayer

After the infant is baptised a baptismal card is issued. This is an official record that the baptism has taken place.

BELIEFS ABOUT BAPTISM

The Church of Ireland describes baptism as:

> "union with Christ in his death and resurrection, the forgiveness of sins, and a new birth into God's family."
>
> *The Revised Catechism*

At baptism, a person receives forgiveness and a new life in Christ and becomes part of Christ's body, the Church. This begins the journey of the Christian life. When the child is old enough to understand they can take their own vows at a service of confirmation.

SYMBOLISM OF BAPTISM

1. Water

Water symbolises cleansing from sin and the beginning of New Life.

2. The Sign of the Cross

The minister makes the sign of the cross on the infant's forehead during the baptism, as a visible sign of belonging to Christ: "Christ claims you for his own. Receive the sign of the cross. Live as a disciple of Christ" (*Book of Common Prayer*, page 362).

3. White Garment

In the Church of Ireland, the baby is usually clothed in a white garment. In baptism they have "*become clothed in Christ*" (Galatians 3:27). It is a sign of happiness, new life, innocence and sinlessness.

BAPTISM IN THE BAPTIST CHURCH

There are three main points to remember about baptism in the Baptist Church. These will be considered in more detail in the following section:

1. Baptism is considered to be an ordinance, not a sacrament.
2. It is for believing Christians only.
3. It is by total immersion in water.

Who is baptised?

Baptist Churches do not baptise infants. They argue that a person wanting to be baptised should be a professing Christian, and should be old enough to understand why there is a need for baptism. The type of baptism carried out in the Baptist church is called 'believers' baptism'. The youngest people who are baptised in the Baptist Church have usually reached secondary school age.

A ceremony of baptism in the Baptist Church

In the Baptist church baptism always takes place in public because it is a public confession of faith in Christ. Those to be baptised invite friends and family. The ceremony usually happens at the end of a Sunday worship service. The ceremony includes the following parts:

The baptismal tank is opened and the pastor, dressed in casual clothes, will get into the tank, which is filled waist deep in water.

The candidate receives a Certificate of Baptism which gives details of the name of the person baptised, the date, the pastor's name and the name of the local church.

BELIEFS ABOUT BAPTISM

Baptists do not believe that there is any special power or presence of God during the ceremony of Baptism. It is simply symbolic. Baptism was instituted and ordained by Jesus for the church, to strengthen believers. For this reason, Baptists refer to baptism as an **ordinance**, not a **sacrament**.

After baptism the person becomes a full member of the church. It is a serious commitment, and a way of formalising a person's faith. Baptism is considered 'outward expression of an inward change', and a clear commitment to turn from sinful ways.

SYMBOLISM OF BAPTISM

Baptists believe that baptism should be by **total immersion**:

> "Immersion, or dipping of the person in water, is necessary to the due administration of this ordinance."
>
> *Things Most Surely Believed among Us, The Baptist Confession of Faith, with Scripture Proofs, of 1689*

The person being baptised will follow the pastor into the tank. Normally, men wear a white shirt and trousers and women wear a special robe.

The Pastor will ask the candidate for baptism:

> *"Do you now confess Jesus Christ as your Lord and Saviour?"*

The candidate answers:

> *"I do"*

The candidate may now take the opportunity to tell those gathered about how they became a Christian and why they want to be baptised.

The candidate for baptism clasps their hands in front of their chest. The pastor puts one of his hands on the person's hands and the other one behind the person's back. The pastor then says:

> *"On profession of your faith in the Lord Jesus Christ as your personal Saviour, I now baptise you in the name of the Father and of the Son and of the Holy Spirit. Amen."*

The pastor then plunges the person under the water until they are completely immersed, and immediately pulls the person out of the water again.

The newly baptised person then climbs up the steps and leaves the tank to go and get changed. The congregation sings a hymn. The baptism is followed by a celebration of the Lord's Supper.

In the Baptist tradition, the symbolism of baptism reflects Paul's teaching in Romans 6:3–5:

> "For surely you know that when we were baptised into union with Christ Jesus, we were baptised into union with his death. By our baptism, then, we were buried with him and shared his death, in order that, just as Christ was raised from death by the glorious power of the Father, so also we might live a new life. For since we have become one with him in dying as he did, in the same way we shall be one with him by being raised to life as he was."

- Being immersed under the water = dying to old, sinful way of life
- Being under the water = being buried with Christ
- Coming out of the water = rising to a new life in Christ

BAPTISM IN THE METHODIST CHURCH

There are three main points about baptism in the Methodist Church. These will be considered in more detail in the following section:

1. Baptism is a sacrament.
2. It is for the infants of believers or for children and adults who were not baptised as infants.
3. It is carried out by pouring or sprinkling water over the person's head.

Baptism by immersion is a symbol of sharing in the death, burial and resurrection of Christ.

The physical falling back into the water is a symbolic burial. This is a sign of change and repentance (turning from your sins). The change is so drastic that the old person is 'buried'.

The rising up out of the water is a symbol of resurrection. The old, sinful self is buried, and the new self is alive.

The message of life change is clear. It is as if the person is saying: "my old life is behind me – I am a new person, with a new life."

Is Baptism necessary for new members of the Baptist Church?

Some people who were baptised as children might move churches and want to join a local Baptist congregation. Normally, Baptist churches do not require them to be rebaptised, as long as they have made another adult declaration of faith, such as confirmation in the Church of Ireland.

Who is baptised?

The children of Christian parents are usually baptised as infants in the Methodist Church. The *Methodist Service Book* also explains that older children and adults can also receive the sacrament of baptism.

The Role of Sponsors

In the Methodist Church parents can bring relatives and family friends to act as sponsors. The church also provides a sponsor, usually someone involved in children's ministry. During the ceremony they promise to support the parents in bringing the child up in the faith. It is considered a privilege and a responsibility.

A CEREMONY OF BAPTISM IN THE METHODIST CHURCH

Baptisms take place in public, usually during the Sunday morning worship service. This is because at baptism a child is welcomed into the fellowship of the church. The order of the baptismal service is set out in the *Methodist Service Book*.

The parents and sponsors bring the child to the font, where the Bible is read.

The congregation promise to

> *"maintain the common life of worship and service that he/she and all children among you may grow in grace and in the knowledge and love of God and of his Son Jesus Christ."*

The parents promise to bring the child up in the way of Christ by teaching and guiding the child in Christian ways.

The minister asks the child's name and makes the sign of the cross on its forehead using water from the font:

> *"(Name), I baptise you in the Name of the Father, and of the Son and of the Holy Spirit."*

The child may be presented with a Bible as a reminder of the baptism.

In some cases a lit candle may be presented by the church sponsor with the words:

> *"I give you this sign, for you now belong to Christ, the light of the world."*

The minister will then pray for the child and their family.

BELIEFS ABOUT BAPTISM

In the Methodist Church baptism is a sign and seal that a person has become a member of God's family, the Church.

The child is too young to even realise the power of God's love, and it is hoped that when the child is older they will make a personal profession of faith and agree to live by their baptismal vows. Methodists believe that it is possible to be a Christian without being baptised.

SYMBOLISM OF BAPTISM

1. Water

Water symbolises cleansing from sin and the beginning of New Life.

2. The Sign of the Cross

The minister makes the sign of the cross on the infant's forehead during the baptism, as a sign that they belong to Christ.

3. Candle

This is a symbol that the child belongs to Christ, the Light of the World, and is invited to 'shine', as Jesus directed in Matthew 5:16.

BAPTISM IN THE PRESBYTERIAN CHURCH

There are three main points about baptism in the Presbyterian Church. These will be considered in more detail in the following section:

1. Baptism is a sacrament.
2. It is for the infants of believers or for adults who were not baptised as infants.
3. It is usually carried out by sprinkling water over the person's head.

Who is baptised?

Presbyterians baptise infants, although people can be baptised as adults. A minister can refuse to baptise if he feels the parents do not meet certain criteria: They must be practicing Christians and regular church attenders.

A CEREMONY OF BAPTISM IN THE PRESBYTERIAN CHURCH

Baptism takes place in public in front of the local congregation. It usually forms part of a normal Sunday morning service

The parents and minister stand at the font. The minister asks the parents two questions:

> *"In presenting this child for baptism do you profess your faith in God as your Creator and Father, in Jesus Christ as your Lord and Saviour, and in the Holy Spirit as you Sanctifier and Guide?"*

> *"Will you, by God's help, provide a Christian home and bring up this child in the worship and teaching of the church, so that your child may come to know Jesus Christ as Lord and Saviour?"*

The parents answer, "We do".

The minister holds the child and makes the sign of the cross on its forehead using water from the font:

> *"In the name of the Father, the Son and the Holy Spirit, I baptise you (name of child)."*

> *"We now receive this child into the fellowship of the Church and promise to order our congregational life that he/she may grow up in the knowledge and love of God."*

The congregation then sings the Aaronic Blessing to welcome the child into the fellowship of the church:

> *"The Lord bless you and keep you. The Lord make his face to shine upon you and be gracious onto you. The Lord lift up his countenance upon you and give you peace."*

BELIEFS ABOUT BAPTISM

Presbyterians do not believe that baptism makes a child a Christian. Rather, it is a sign to show the work of the grace of God. Presbyterians believe that what matters most in baptism is what God is doing for his people – and not what they do. Infant baptism looks forward to a time when the child will have his or her own personal faith.

Presbyterians understand baptism as an outward sign of entering into a **Covenant** with God (see page 23). In the Old Testament the Covenant with God was sealed with the physical sign of circumcision (Genesis 17:10). The Covenant changed with Christ, and so did the symbol– from circumcision to baptism.

Just as whole households were circumcised to mark themselves out as being in Covenant with God, so Presbyterians baptise whole households to mark them out as being in Covenant with God through Jesus.

Through baptism the child becomes a member of the Church, the body of Christ.

SYMBOLISM OF BAPTISM

Water

Baptism is carried out by pouring or sprinkling water on the person. This was the main way that ceremonial purification was carried out in the Old Testament.

Presbyterians believe that just as water makes people clean, so baptism pictures how God, through Jesus Christ, can make a person's whole life clean, forgiving their sins and giving new life in the Holy Spirit.

Blessing

The Aaronic Blessing is a priestly blessing from the Old Testament (Numbers 6:24–26). The congregation sing it as a way of welcoming the new child into the congregation.

FOR YOUR FOLDER

1. Name two places where a baptism can take place.
2. Describe a baptismal ceremony in a denomination of your choice.
3. With reference to at least two denominations, explain why most churches have baptismal ceremonies.
4. How does Christian baptism reflect Biblical teaching?
5. Explain the difference in the meaning of baptism for the Catholic tradition and one Protestant tradition.
6. Some people have a big family celebration following a baptism. Do you think that it is wrong for baptism to become a social rather than a religious event?
7. Do you think that it is important for a Christian to be baptised? Give reasons for your answer.

BELIEVERS' BAPTISM VERSUS INFANT BAPTISM

The debate about how baptism should be performed has been going on for centuries. Most Christian churches baptise both infants and adults, but some believe that baptism should only be for adults.

The Catholic Church, Church of Ireland, Presbyterian Church and Methodist Church all practice baptism for both infants and adults. They recognise baptism performed in any of these denominations as valid, subject to certain conditions. It is only possible to be baptised once, so people who change denomination are not baptised again.

ARGUMENTS FOR BELIEVER'S BAPTISM

The Baptist church, and some other groups, do not accept infant baptism at all. They have three main arguments:

1. Believer's baptism is the only kind of baptism seen in the New Testament.

2. Baptism cannot make someone a Christian. It is an outward sign of inward change.

3. Infants are not old enough to understand what they are doing. Baptism is only meaningful if it is a personal choice.

In the New Testament, baptism is a sign that someone has been changed and wants to follow Christ. Baptism is for those who have turned away from their sin and put their faith in the Lord Jesus Christ, and who are committed to living his way.

People should be baptised because it is the command of Christ:

> "Go and make disciples of all nations, baptising them in the name of the Father, the Son and the Holy Spirit" (Matthew 28.19).

From the very beginning, the Church has baptised those who want to follow Jesus (Acts 2:38–41).

Baptism should be by full immersion in water. This was the practice in the New Testament and it best symbolises the death, burial and resurrection of Jesus with which Christians are identifying. Examples can be found in Matthew 3:16, Acts 8:38 and Romans 6:1–4. The Greek word *baptizo* used in these texts means 'to dip' or to 'submerge'.

Although churches that support infant baptism would say otherwise, there is no conclusive evidence of infant baptism occuring in the Bible.

ARGUMENTS FOR INFANT BAPTISM

Infant baptism is practiced in the Church of Ireland and the Presbyterian, Methodist and Catholic churches. Each has a slightly different understanding of baptism, but all agree that baptism is the ceremony which brings new babies into the community of faith. The main arguments for infant baptism are explained below:

1. Baptism is a sign of becoming part of the Christian community and beginning a spiritual journey, so it is appropriate that people are baptised as children.

2. Baptism is a Sacrament in which people

experience God's grace. Children should not be excluded from these experiences.

3. There is evidence of infant baptism in the Bible.

For Presbyterians especially, the Old Testament symbolism of Covenant is an important part of baptism. From Genesis 17:10 onwards the people used circumcision to mark themselves out as God's people. Jewish boys are circumcised when they are eight days old as a sign of the Covenant with God. Likewise, the children of Christian parents are baptised as a sign of being God's people under the **New Covenant** (see page 24).

In Genesis 17:9–14 it was commanded that every male in the **whole household** should be circumcised. Likewise, there is evidence of 'Household Baptism' in the New Testament, notably in Acts 16:15 and Acts 16:31–33. Churches that teach adult baptism only would argue that these verses are inconclusive.

Catholic view:

For Catholics, baptism is the beginning of the faith journey. Through baptism, children become members of God's family, the Church; are cleansed from original sin; and receive God's grace and the Holy Spirit.

Throughout their lives, the baptised person will continue to grow and receive God's grace through other sacraments at key times in the their life. For example, the sacrament of Confirmation as they begin the journey into adulthood; the sacrament of Marriage or Holy Orders; the sacrament of Anointing the Sick when they are ill.

It is argued that the child will benefit from being brought up in the faith of their parents and from belonging to a believing community.

While an infant is unable to make baptismal promises for themselves, everyone has the chance to renew the promises every year, during the Sacrament of Confirmation at the Easter Vigil.

DEBATE

INFANT BAPTISM VERSUS BELIEVER'S BAPTISM. Look at the cases for infant baptism and believers' baptism.

Summarise the main points of each argument, including Bible references.

Organise a class debate on which form of baptism is more acceptable.

IN A GROUP

Some of the reasons Christians give for baptism are influenced by the preference for either infant or believers' baptism.

Look at each of the following reasons in turn and discuss whether each supports infant baptism, believers' baptism or both:

Reasons for Baptism

It grants salvation

It takes away sin

It commemorates Christ's death and Resurrection

It fulfils Jesus' command to baptise

It confers God's grace

It is a public expression of faith

FOR YOUR FOLDER

1. Explain the difference between infant baptism and believer's baptism.

2. "It is the responsibility of all Christian parents to make sure that their children are baptised as babies."
   Do you agree or disagree? Give reasons for your answer showing that you have considered different points of view.

4. Do you think that the promises made in baptism should be publicly renewed on a regular basis? Give reasons for your answer.

EUCHARIST OR COMMUNION

Eucharist or Communion refers to a symbolic meal of bread and wine which is the most important ceremony in the Christian Church. It remembers the Last Supper that Jesus ate with his disciples where he made the bread and wine symbols of his death (See page 36). On that occasion Jesus gave thanks for the bread and wine before sharing it with his disciples. The word *eucharist* is a Greek word which means 'thanksgiving'. When Christians celebrate the Eucharist they are thanking God for all he has done for them.

The celebration of the Eucharist involves the blessing and eating of bread and wine (called the 'elements'), although the different denominations have their own beliefs about what happens during this act of worship.

> **The various Christian denominations refer to this symbolic meal by different names.**
>
> **Catholic Church**
> Eucharist or Mass
>
> **Church of Ireland and Methodist**
> Holy Communion
>
> **Baptist**
> The Lord's Supper or The Breaking of Bread
>
> **Presbyterian**
> The Lord's Supper or Communion

SYMBOLISM OF BREAD AND WINE

At the Last Supper Jesus took the symbols of the **Passover meal** and gave them new meaning.

As Passover celebrated the Covenant between God and His people, Jesus' death made a **New Covenant** between God and His people. That New Covenant is remembered in the Eucharist.

Passover remembers how God set the people free from slavery in Egypt. Christians celebrate how God has set them free from sin.

On the first Passover God instructed the people to sacrifice a lamb. At the sign of its blood, death would 'pass over' and leave them unharmed. Christians believe that Christ's sacrifice means that they will not die, but have eternal life.

As the blood of a lamb sealed the Old Covenant, the blood of Jesus sealed the New Covenant. This is why Jesus is sometimes referred to as 'the lamb of God'.

The symbol of bread has layers of meaning:

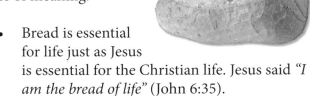

- Bread is essential for life just as Jesus is essential for the Christian life. Jesus said *"I am the bread of life"* (John 6:35).

- Bread was the food of the poor and was easily available to all, just as Jesus is available to all who seek him with a sincere heart.

- In order for bread to be made the grain of wheat must be crushed, so bread becomes a powerful symbol of death and the sacrifice of Jesus' life.

- In the Eucharist the bread is broken, symbolising that Jesus body was physically broken.

The wine is also symbolic:

- At Passover, wine was a sign of God's blessing on His people. Jesus is God's blessing on His people.

- The colour of wine was an appropriate symbol of the blood that Jesus shed.

- In order for the wine to be made the grape must be crushed, so wine becomes a symbol of death and the sacrifice of Jesus' life.

TEACHER'S NOTE

For this section you should study the practice of Eucharist or Communion in the Catholic Church and one Protestant tradition: Church of Ireland, Baptist, Methodist or Presbyterian.

(Continue reading from page 114.)

THE SACRAMENT OF EUCHARIST IN THE CATHOLIC CHURCH

The service of Eucharist is usually called the **Mass**. Mass is celebrated every day in the Catholic Church and most Catholics attend Mass every Sunday. All Catholics who have been baptised and who have made the Sacrament of Reconciliation (confession) can receive the Eucharist. It is the central act of worship in the Catholic Church.

Transubstantiation

Catholics believe that the elements of bread and wine are transformed into the body and blood of Christ through the act of **consecration**.

The Catholic Church teaches that:

"…We know ourselves to be bound by the command the Lord gave on the eve of his Passion: 'Do this in remembrance of me.' We carry out this command of the Lord by celebrating the memorial of his sacrifice. In so doing we offer to the Father what he had given to us: the gifts of his creation, bread and wine, which by the power of the Holy Spirit and by the words of Christ, have become the body and blood of Christ. Christ is thus really and mysteriously made present."

Bread only

Unlike other Christian traditions, Catholics usually receive only the bread at Mass. There are a number of reasons for this:

- Catholics believe that once the bread and wine have been blessed the presence of Christ is in them. They should be treated as sacred. If someone drops a communion wafer it can be picked up, but this is not the case with spilled wine.
- In the crucifixion, Jesus' blood was separated from His body. At the Resurrection, his body and blood were no longer separate but one.
- When the bread and wine are consecrated they both become Christ. This means that when Catholics receive the bread they do receive the whole Christ, body and blood.
- The priest receives both bread and wine (called 'Communion under both kinds')

Ceremony of the Eucharist

- The people recall their sins and express sorrow for them in the **Penitential Rite**.

- The priest or a member of the congregation reads from the Bible in the **Liturgy of the Word.**

- The congregation say the **Creed** and the **Prayers of the Faithful.**

- If it is a Sunday, a collection of money will be taken, and offered up with the bread and wine in the **offertory procession.**

- The Priest will read the **Preface** and the **Eucharistic Prayer.** The central part of this is the **Consecration** of the bread and wine to become the body and blood of Christ.

- The **'Our Father'** is said followed by the **'Lamb of God'** prayer which emphasises Christ's sacrifice for the forgiveness of sins.

- The congregation process to the altar to receive the body and blood of Christ under the appearance of **bread and wine**. Usually, only the bread is distributed to the congregation.

- The priest ends the Mass with a **blessing** and a command to go out "to love and serve the Lord."

(The whole service is explored in more detail on page 55)

BELIEFS ABOUT MASS

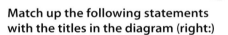

IN A GROUP

Match up the following statements with the titles in the diagram (right:)

- Jesus commanded his disciples to *"Do this in memory of me"* at the last Supper. Christians obey this command.

- The mass brings the whole community together as well as bringing the believer and Christ into closer relationship.

- Catholics receive the body and blood of Christ under the appearance of bread and wine.

- *"Take this and eat. This is my body which is broken for you. Take this and drink. This is my blood which is poured out for you for the forgiveness of sins."*

- When Catholics celebrate the Mass they remember the words and actions of Jesus at the last Supper.

- The Mass is *eucharist*.

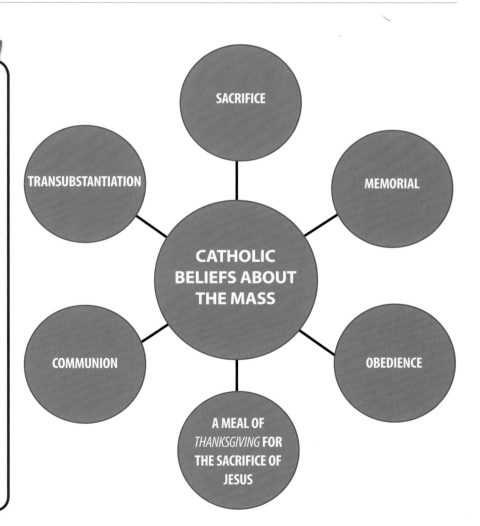

SACRIFICE

TRANSUBSTANTIATION

MEMORIAL

CATHOLIC BELIEFS ABOUT THE MASS

OBEDIENCE

COMMUNION

A MEAL OF *THANKSGIVING* **FOR THE SACRIFICE OF JESUS**

THE REVELATION OF GOD AND THE CHRISTIAN CHURCH

HOLY COMMUNION IN THE CHURCH OF IRELAND

In the Church of Ireland Holy Communion is celebrated on most Sundays. Communion is normally taken for the first time after Confirmation, usually at around 14 years old, when the individual decides to take on the baptismal vows for themselves.

A Ceremony of Holy Communion

- After greeting the congregation the rector says a preparation prayer (a **collect for purity**), which is followed by a hymn of praise.

- A member of the congregation will read from the Bible and then the rector will give the sermon.

- The congregation recites **the Apostles' Creed**.

- There are prayers of **intercession**, a reading of the commandments, prayers of **confession** and **absolution**.

- The **prayer of humble access** prepares people's hearts and minds to receive the sacrament.

- The congregation will share the **sign of peace**, shaking hands with each other and saying something like "The peace of the Lord be with you."

- An offering of money is taken to the altar where the bread and wine for communion are also placed.

- The rector takes the bread and wine in his hands and blesses them. He says a prayer of thanksgiving and the congregation respond by saying the **Lord's Prayer**.

- The rector breaks the bread and says "The bread which we break is a sharing in the body of Christ."

- The congregation replies with the words,

"We, being many, are one body for we all share in the one bread."

- The people move from their seats to kneel at the altar rail. The rector or his assistants put a small piece of bread into people's hands, and everyone takes a sip out of a common cup of wine.

- The rector says to each person "The body of Christ keep you in eternal life" and "The blood of Christ keep you in eternal life."

- There is a prayer of thanksgiving and commitment to serve Christ.

- The rector ends the service with a blessing: "Go in peace to love and serve the Lord." The congregation answers, "In the name of Christ. Amen."

What does the Church of Ireland believe about Holy Communion?

A WAY TO REMEMBER THE DEATH OF CHRIST

CHURCH OF IRELAND BELIEFS ABOUT COMMUNION

A WAY TO ANTICIPATE THE COMING OF CHRIST'S KINGDOM

A CELEBRATION OF CHRIST'S RESURRECTION AND ASCENSION

IN A GROUP

Match up the following explanations with the statements in the diagram above:

- During the celebration of Holy Communion Christians remember Jesus' death on the cross.

- Communion celebrates that Jesus rose from the dead and ascended into heaven.

- At communion Christians look forward to the Second Coming of Christ on Earth.

THE LORD'S SUPPER IN THE BAPTIST CHURCH

Baptists allow anyone who is a Christian to celebrate The Lord's Supper in their church. It does not matter what denomination they belong to or what age they are. The term for this is an 'open table'.

Communion is usually celebrated once a week, at the end of the morning worship service, although in some Baptist Churches there is an evening celebration of the Lord's Supper once a month. It is a very informal time of sharing in the Baptist Church, although it is also considered to be a serious and reverent act of worship.

A Ceremony of the Lord's Supper

- After the morning worship service ends there is a time of quietness for people to think about the communion celebration they are about to participate in.

- The pastor will invite all present to share in an informal time of worship. Those present may choose a hymn or chorus for everyone to sing together.

- A member of the congregation may choose a Bible reading or pray to focus on the death and resurrection of Christ.

- Someone will say a prayer of thanks for the bread.

- Then bread is passed around by **deacons** so that everyone present can take a piece. Once everyone has been served, they all eat their bread at the same time.

- The same procedure is carried out for the wine.

- A period of quietness follows for people to reflect.

- Finally the Pastor prays and gives a word of blessing.

What do Baptists believe about the Lord's Supper?

A WAY OF OBEYING CHRIST

A WITNESS FOR CHRIST

BELIEFS ABOUT THE LORD'S SUPPER

A WAY TO REMEMBER CHRIST

A REMINDER OF CHRIST'S RETURN

A WAY TO IDENTIFY IN CHRIST'S DEATH AND RESURRECTION

IN A GROUP

Match up the following explanations with the statements in the diagram above:

-At the Last Supper Jesus told his disciples "Do this in remembrance of me" (1 Corinthians 11:24). By celebrating the Lord's Supper Baptists believe they are obeying Christ.

-The bread and wine are symbols of Christ's body and blood. Baptists believe that the Lord's Supper is a memorial of the death of Christ on the cross.

-Baptists believe that when a person becomes a Christian they experience a death to their old, sinful way of life and that there is a spiritual rebirth or resurrection.

-By celebrating the Lord's Supper, Baptists believe that they are telling the world that they believe in Christ, that he died on the cross for the sin of the world and that through Christ's death there is salvation (being saved from sin).

-When Baptists celebrate communion they 'proclaim the Lord's death until he comes.' This refers to the belief in the Second Coming of Christ.

HOLY COMMUNION IN THE METHODIST CHURCH

Holy Communion is celebrated at least once a month in the Methodist church. It usually takes place during the worship service but can sometimes also occur in a more informal way, for example, at a Bible study.

Methodists allow anyone who is a Christian to celebrate Holy Communion in their church. It does not matter what denomination they belong to or what age they are. The term for this is an 'open table'.

The minister will invite "those who love Him (the Lord) or who would like to love Him more" to participate in the celebration.

The wine used for communion is always non-alcoholic.

A Ceremony of Holy Communion in the Methodist Church

- Communion takes place following the **Ministry of the Word** (Bible readings and sermon).

- The congregation will recite the **Nicene Creed** together. This is to show that they are united with other churches.

- The congregation will **share the peace**, shaking hands with each other and saying something like "The peace of the Lord be with you."

- Cloths are removed from the bread and wine which are already on the communion table.

- The congregation says a prayer of thanksgiving for what Christ has done and to look forward to his return.

- The minister takes the bread, breaks it and invites the congregation to come forward, out of their seats, to receive the bread and wine.

- The people kneel at the communion rail and receive the elements of bread and wine from the minister and his stewards.

- When everyone has received communion the elements of bread and wine are covered up again by cloths and the people go back to their seats.

- The minister prays and, after a hymn, announces the **benediction** – a word of blessing.

What do Methodists believe about Holy Communion?

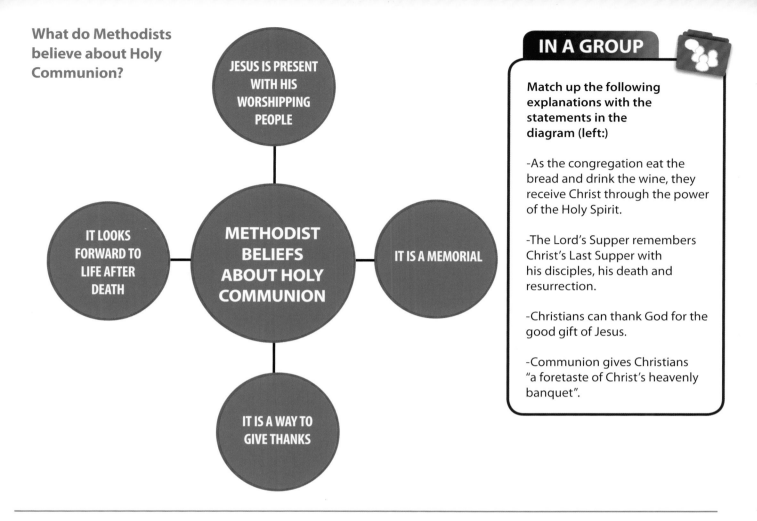

IN A GROUP

Match up the following explanations with the statements in the diagram (left:)

-As the congregation eat the bread and drink the wine, they receive Christ through the power of the Holy Spirit.

-The Lord's Supper remembers Christ's Last Supper with his disciples, his death and resurrection.

-Christians can thank God for the good gift of Jesus.

-Communion gives Christians "a foretaste of Christ's heavenly banquet".

COMMUNION IN THE PRESBYTERIAN CHURCH

Communion is celebrated between two and six times a year in the Presbyterian Church. A pre-communion service is held on the Wednesday before Communion Sunday to help people to prepare for the sacrament. New church members are also formally welcomed at this service.

Anyone who professes to be a Christian is invited to celebrate communion in the Presbyterian Church. Children do not take communion. Teenagers who feel ready to celebrate the sacrament do so after a discussion with the minister and usually attend communion classes beforehand as well.

Presbyterians keep a record of those who take communion through the use of communion tokens. These little cards are filled out with each member's name and put into a basket on Communion Sunday. This is a useful record when it comes to times for the voting of new elders. It also can be used to provide information on who is no longer taking communion. The minister or elder may go to visit such people to make sure there are no problems.

A Ceremony of Communion in the Presbyterian Church

- Communion takes place in a normal Sunday service, morning or evening, after the sermon.
- The minister opens in prayer
- The minister reads an appropriate passage from the New Testament, such as Matthew 26:27–29 or 1 Corinthians 11:23–25.

- The minister stands in front of the communion table and prays a blessing on the bread and wine.

- The bread and wine are given out to the congregation by elders.

- The bread is usually small pieces or shortbread served on a plate that is passed around the pews.

- The wine is non-alcoholic, served in small individual glasses to each person.

- In some Presbyterian churches everyone waits until all people have been served and then take communion together.

- The minister says a prayer of thanksgiving.

- Everyone stands to sing a hymn.

- The service ends when the minister announces the benediction – a word of blessing.

What do Presbyterians believe about Holy Communion?

REMEMBRANCE

EXPECTATION

THANKSGIVING

PRESBYTERIAN BELIEFS ABOUT COMMUNION

NOURISHMENT

FELLOWSHIP AND SHARING

DEDICATION

TESTIMONY

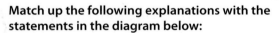

IN A GROUP

Match up the following explanations with the statements in the diagram below:

Communion helps Christians to remember the death of Christ.

-Christians have an opportunity to thank God and praise him for the death of Christ.

-By taking communion, the faith of Christians is built up.

-Christians take communion in the company of other believers and share in the fellowship of the Christian family.

-Communion is a way for Christians to renew their commitment to Christ.

-Christians look forward to the second coming of Christ.

-By taking communion Christians are declaring in a public way that they follow Christ.

FOR YOUR FOLDER

1. Describe the service of communion/Eucharist in a denomination of your choice.

2. How does a communion service remind people about events in the life of Jesus?

3. What are some of the main differences in belief and practice of communion in the two denominations you have studied.

4. For what reasons do Christians take part in the act of communion?

5. "You cannot celebrate communion/eucharist too often." Do you agree or disagree? Give reasons for your answer.

Chapter 10

THE ROLE OF THE CHURCH IN CONTEMPORARY SOCIETY

THE CONTRIBUTION OF THE CHRISTIAN CHURCHES TO PEACE AND RECONCILIATION IN A DIVIDED SOCIETY

Northern Ireland could be described as a 'divided society' in terms of both religion and politics. Christianity is the main religion in Northern Ireland but there is a history of division and conflict between groups of Catholics and Protestants. Similarly in politics there has been considerable conflict between Unionists (those supporting union with Britain) and Nationalists (those in favour of a United Ireland). Many of you will be used to seeing territorial markings such as painted kerbstones and the flying of national flags.

Over the years, churches in Northern Ireland have made a substantial contribution to reconciliation between the Protestant and Catholic communities.

IN A GROUP

1. What do you know about the period of history in Northern Ireland that is referred to as 'The Troubles'?
2. Have you ever taken part in cross-community projects?

FURTHER THINKING

Find out about cross community projects in your school, church or area.

The Corrymeela Community

The Corrymeela Community was founded in 1965 by the Rev. Ray Davey, chaplain at Queen's University, Belfast. It is a group of Christians in Ireland, both Protestant and Catholic, who believe they are called together as the 'Instrument of God's Peace' in the Church and the world. Corrymeela was set up to encourage reconciliation and peace-building in Northern Ireland, through the healing of social, religious and political divisions.

Throughout the period known as 'The Troubles', the Corrymeela Community worked with individuals and communities that suffered through violence and division caused by the Northern Irish conflict. It continues to encourage positive relationships between all kinds of people by:

- providing a safe place for people to express themselves
- providing the opportunity for dialogue between people from contrasting religious traditions
- supporting victims of violence and injustice

CORRYMEELA: PROJECTS AND ACTIVITIES

Corrymeela runs three centres in Belfast, Ballycastle, and Glenshesk.

Corrymeela Centre, Ballycastle

The centre has facilities for over 100 residents allowing people the chance to stay and enjoy picturesque surroundings while participating in programmes:

- Work with schools focuses on community relations issues, often through citizenship
- Family work
- Work with church communities, in their own faith, and to support meeting people from other religious traditions
- Youth work, primarily focused on marginalised young people (those who are outsiders).
- Community work looking at issues of inter-community relations, and cross-community work.
- Sanctuary and support for victims and those under stress
- 'Treetops' children's bereavement support group

Knocklayd

Situated on the slopes of Knocklayd Mountain in Antrim, this centre offers a place of retreat and respite for groups of up to 16 while encouraging 'ecumenical spirituality'.

Corrymeela House, Belfast

Corrymeela House functions as an administrative office and meeting place for Corrymeela groups in the city.

NOTE

'ECUMENICAL' – promoting unity between different Christian denominations.

1. What is the Corrymeela Community?
2. Explain how the Corrymeela community encourages positive relationships between all kinds of people.
3. Give four examples of the work carried out at the Corrymeela centres.
4. Do you think that the kind of cross-community relationship developed at Corrymeela are valuable? Give reasons for your answer.

FURTHER THINKING

Find out about some of the personal stories from people who have been helped by the Corrymeela Community from their website: www.corrymeela.org

The Advantages of Cross-Community projects:

- It provides a platform for re-examining the differences that have divided Christians and created mistrust.

- Honest and open discussion of all areas of faith are encouraged. Christians learn **to disagree without being disagreeable.**

- People can gradually learn about the other tradition, its spiritual strengths and weaknesses.

- **Strangers become friends.** People can socialise together and enjoy each other's culture.

- Protestants and Catholics realise how important Christ is in each other's faith-tradition; and discover just how much truth they have **in common**.

- Christians can be united in worship

- It shows other congregations of the Church, Catholic and Protestant, the value of such contact between the two traditions.

FURTHER THINKING

You can find out about the work of The Cornerstone Community from their website: www.cornerstonecommunity.co.uk

IN A GROUP

Look up the verses and complete the table explaining the relevance of the teaching for reconciliation:

Biblical Teaching	Teaching for today
Galatians 3:28	Most Christians today would say that this means there is no difference between Catholic or Protestant, black or white, man or woman, settled person or traveller.
Acts 17:26	
Matthew 22:39	
Genesis 1:26–27	

THE CONTRIBUTION OF THE CHRISTIAN CHURCH TO LOCAL COMMUNITY AND COMMUNITY COHESION

We have seen how religious differences have caused social division in the past; however, many churches and Christian groups work to bring the community together and create cohesion. The word 'cohesion' means 'holding together'.

In the past, when more people attended church services, the local church was often the heart of the community. In some places, social and community life still revolves around the church. The Church is a community of people and they aim to spread the benefits of that community to those around them. This is often referred to as 'outreach'.

Outreach can simply mean that individual Christians aim to form good relationships with people they meet, but churches and other Christian groups can organise events and activities that benefit the wider community around them.

For example:

- **Youth work**
  Most churches have some form of organised youth work such as Youth Clubs, Scouts and Guides, Boy's Brigade and Girl's Brigade, football clubs, drop-in centres and Church Schools.

- **Clubs and societies**
  Some churches run a wide range of clubs and societies as varied as bowling, photography, flower-arranging, film nights, painting classes and discussion groups. These are open to anyone, and aim to create community cohesion and good relationships.

- **Support groups**
  Depending on the resources available to them, some local churches are able to offer free professional support and advice such as family planning or counselling, and run groups like Alcoholics Anonymous.

- **Worship Services**
  Sunday Morning services create community cohesion as people worship together and become part of a church family. Most churches make efforts to make the service as accessible and welcoming as possible for newcomers.

- **Supporting other projects**
  Some churches offer practical help to other organisations that work in the community like homeless shelters or care programmes.

CHURCH PROJECTS

Embrace NI

Embrace NI is a group of Christians who have come together to support asylum seekers and refugees in Northern Ireland, particularly those who are homeless or are out of work. Some churches support its work by collecting clothes and toiletries for distribution. Others work for the organisation providing information, training and resources to encourage church communities to welcome people from minority ethnic backgrounds.

Interfaith

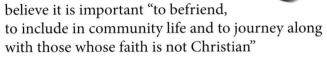

Ireland, has become a multi-faith island. Christians live alongside Muslims, Hindus, Jews, Buddhists, Humanists and others. Many denominations, for example the Methodist Church, believe it is important "to befriend, to include in community life and to journey along with those whose faith is not Christian"

(Irish Methodism and Inter-Faith Understanding; Report to Conference 2007).

Storehouse

Storehouse is a project to provide food parcels for struggling families across Belfast. People can donate food and volunteer to help packing in the warehouse or distributing the food. The project was started by Belfast City Vineyard, and a number of other local churches soon got involved.

Nightlight

Nightlight is an outreach project run by the Presbyterian Church. On the busy streets of Belfast every Friday and Saturday night, volunteers spend time giving out tea, talking, and offering practical help to partygoers and the homeless.

SVP

The Catholic charity 'The Society of St Vincent de Paul' is the largest, voluntary, charitable organisation in Ireland. It has been helping to alleviate poverty and work for social justice in Northern Ireland since 1848. The aim of the Society is: "to enhance the quality of life for those in need, regardless of creed, colour or caste".

Volunteers offer friendship, support, advice and practical help to families, pensioners and individuals each week. Some examples of the services offered by St Vincent de Paul include:

- Cash assistance
- Food and clothing
- Shops and internet cafes
- Furniture Stores
- Breakfast and Afterschool clubs
- Crèche
- Playgroup
- Mother and Toddler Group
- Centre for the Deaf (Belfast)
- Drop-in centres
- Resource centres
- Providing accommodation to vulnerable people
- Holiday schemes
- Holiday Home (Newcastle)

With 179 branches across Northern Ireland, individuals can get involved as volunteers. Churches, clubs and schools can help by fundraising with bake sales, auctions, sponsored sports days or whatever they can come up with.

Pupils at Our Lady and Saint Patrick's College Belfast hold a cake sale to raise money for the work of SVP.

FOR YOUR FOLDER

1. What is the aim of the St. Vincent de Paul Society?
2. Give four examples of the kind of work they do.

IN A GROUP

1. How might churches develop ways of reaching out to teenagers and young adults in the community?

2. How can church buildings make a contribution to the life of the local community?

3. What do you think are the main problems facing Christians who want to witness to people on the streets at night?

4. "Christians have nothing to offer young people who just want to go out and have a good time on a Saturday night." Do you agree or disagree? Give reasons for your answer showing you have looked at contrasting points of view.

COMMUNITY SERVICE

One of the ways that Christian schools seek to contribute to community cohesion is through community service programmes.

Dominic explains: "School is about developing the whole person and not just dealing with the academic side of life. Being involved in community service stimulates the students' awareness of the other person's situation and needs, and encourages them to think of a practical response. It also helps develop their sense of empathy.

Community service can sow a seed for later life in appreciating the value of working with others in their wider community who may benefit from their help and friendship.

From a religious faith point of view it enables the young person to fulfill their apostolic calling to put Christian values into action."

Rachel, Maeve and Hannah are involved in community service in the area in which their school is situated. They give up an hour and a half of their own time each week to carry out community service work with 13-17 year olds who have learning difficulties.

Hannah says:
"We had seen older students going out on community service over the years and the satisfaction and enjoyment they got from it. I wanted to be part of it. I work with students who are my own age and I always get a sense of the things I can do which they can't and I feel grateful."

Maeve says:
"It is great to see the joy and excitement in the eyes of the children when we visit. The work is really rewarding. It is a pity we only have an hour and a half every week. I would love to stay longer."

Although the community service programme ends in April. Many people choose to continue their service. I can see why."

Rachel says:
"I didn't know that there were people with special needs so close to the school. I think it is important to give something back to the local community and to become more involved – particularly with people who are less fortunate."

Rachel , Maeve and Hanah were so struck by the needs of the students and the skill and dedication of the teachers at Torbank school that they, led by Maeve, organised a sponsored walk to raise money for equipment . They raised £1000.

IN A GROUP

Make a list of the benefits of being involved in community service.

THE CHALLENGE TO THE CHRISTIAN CHURCH OF CHANGING MORAL, SOCIAL AND CULTURAL VALUES

One of the biggest challenges facing the Christian Church in the 21st century is its attitude to changing moral, social and cultural values. Attitudes towards issues such as sex before marriage, divorce, abortion, euthanasia and war have all faced change in society. This is a major challenge to the Christian Church, which often sees itself having a responsibility to set a moral example in the world.

Christians try to live according to God's standards and the teachings of Jesus and look to the Bible for guidance on moral issues. However, many of the issues that are controversial today are not directly mentioned in the Bible. It is up to the Church to interpret the Bible and to apply its teachings to today's moral issues.

Many Christians accept the traditional opinions of the Church regarding most moral, social and cultural values. Others argue that the church needs to move with the times. They believe the time has come for the church to re-evaluate its opinion on the issues that cause most debate in today's world.

Three issues that cause controversy in the Church today are abortion, euthanasia and homosexuality.

IN A GROUP

"Society's values are moving further away from Biblical ideals."

Do you agree or disagree? Give reasons for your answer.

The issue of Abortion

Many different groups and organisations are debating the rights and wrongs of abortion.

One of the main ethical debates has been about the point at which life begins. When does a group of growing cells count as a human being? Does life begin at conception or birth?

The churches all agree that life begins in the womb, however, they differ on whether or not abortion is ever acceptable. Look at the following church statements:

Denomination	Statement on Abortion
Catholic Church	'Life must be respected with the utmost care from the moment of conception. Abortion and infanticide are abominable crimes.' **Gaudium et Spes 51:3**
Anglican (Church of Ireland)	The Lambeth conference of 1958 received a Committee Report in which it was stated: 'In the strongest terms, Christians reject the practice of induced abortion, or infanticide, which involves the killing of a life already conceived (as well as a violation of the personality of the mother) save at the dictate of strict and undeniable medical necessity.'
Presbyterian Church	'The scriptures leave us in no doubt that from his earliest days in the womb, the unborn child is fully human, a person made in the image of God.' **Leaflet on Abortion, p.1**
Methodist Church	From The Status of the Unborn, a report received by the Methodist Conference 1992: 'The worth of the human race itself hinges on reverence for human life at every stage and the long tradition of Christian teaching is marked by an abhorrence of destroying the life in the womb. But a right to life does not mean an absolute right. Other lives have impinging rights. The life of the mother, whose survival may be crucial because care for the existing family heavily depend upon her, would appear to have priority over that of the foetus, if a choice has to be made...'

FOR YOUR FOLDER

Create a table summarising the attitude of each denomination to abortion based on the information above.

The Issue of Euthanasia

Euthanasia is sometimes known as 'mercy killing' and it refers to the ending of someone's life. It can take the form of actively ending life, such as lethal injections, or simply withholding life-support or medication. One form of Euthanasia, known as 'assisted suicide', has become quite prominent in the media.

Recently, there has been debate about whether all forms of Euthanasia should be illegal and whether people have the right to choose to die, or to request that others end their life.

Many churches have released statements on their position:

Denomination	Statement on Euthanasia
Catholic Church	*'It is necessary to state firmly once more that nothing and no one can in any way permit the killing of an innocent human being, whether a fetus or an embryo, an infant or an adult, an old person, or one suffering from an incurable disease, or a person who is dying. Furthermore, no one is permitted to ask for this act of killing, either for himself or herself or for another person entrusted to his or her care, nor can he or she consent to it, either explicitly or implicitly… What a sick person needs, besides medical care, is love, the human and supernatural warmth with which the sick person can and ought to be surrounded by all those close to him or her, parents and children, doctors and nurses.'* **Declaration on Euthanasia, Sacred Congregation for the Doctrine of the Faith, 1980**
Presbyterian Church	*'Compassion for our fellow human beings means we have the duty to help them die in as comfortable and peaceful ways as we can. We also believe that death is not disaster for those who have committed their lives to Christ. Dying in faith means going to be with him and it is right that we should welcome the release of death for those whose quality of life has been reduced to a daily grind of suffering or infirmity…Above all, the Christian community should take the lead in showing the prayerful, dignified, respectful care which assures people that they are valued and loved, even in the midst of pain and helplessness'.* **Social Issues & Resources Committee**
Anglican (Church of Ireland)	*'…I am not arguing in favour of prolonged suffering… one of the most terrible things that can happen to us, as human beings, is to watch someone we love go through suffering… we can see, at first glance, the reasons why, if someone is suffering terribly with a terminal illness, we might consider euthanasia to be a desirable option…What is needed is not what some are calling, in a horrible travesty of language, the 'therapeutic option' of euthanasia or assisted suicide, but far greater resource – for greater training in palliative care, a care which embraces body, mind and soul.'* **The Bishop of St Albans, Christopher Herbert, commenting in opposition to the Assisted Dying Bill, 2005**

FOR YOUR FOLDER

1. Based on the information above, place the Catholic, Presbyterian and Anglican Churches on the scale below.

Attitude to Euthanasia

Always Wrong   Always Acceptable

2. Based on the table above select a short quotation for each of the Churches, summarising their attitude to euthanasia.

IN A GROUP

1. Explain why the issue of euthanasia causes controversy for the Christian Church.

2. Which denominations are totally against euthanasia?

3. Do you imagine that there will ever be a change of attitude regarding euthanasia among the leadership of these churches?

FURTHER THINKING

What can you find out about the Methodist Church's attitude to euthanasia?

The Issue of Homosexuality

Attitudes to homosexuality have varied throughout history and across culture. Christians aim to base their attitudes and understandings on God's teaching, rather than on the attitudes of those around them, but there is debate on what the church should teach about homosexuality and about the place in the Church of people in homosexual relationships.

Look at the statements below:

Denomination	Statement on Homosexuality
Catholic Church	*'Homosexuality refers to relations between men or between women who experience an exclusive or predominant sexual attraction toward persons of the same sex. …Its psychological genesis remains largely unexplained. Basing itself on Sacred Scripture, which presents homosexual acts as acts of grave depravity, tradition has always declared that 'homosexual acts are intrinsically disordered'…Under no circumstances can they be approved…men and women who have deep-seated homosexual tendencies…must be accepted with respect, compassion, and sensitivity. Every sign of unjust discrimination in their regard should be avoided…'* **The Catechism of the Catholic Church**
Anglican (Church of Ireland)	• *A resolution was passed at the Lambeth Conference in 1998, stating that homosexual acts are 'incompatible with Scripture'. However, it also said this policy would not be the final word.* • *In 2003, the Church of England was prepared to appoint as bishop, Jeffrey John, a priest living in a celibate domestic partnership with another man. Many Anglicans were outraged and the priest decided not to accept the appointment.* • *Many Church of Ireland parishes are opposed to homosexual practice, while others have openly gay parishioners as a matter of routine.*
Presbyterian Church	*'Many teenagers experience same sex attractions. For most these do not linger but are part of their sexual development. For others their sexual development can be arrested by various factors in their upbringing including close family relationships and family breakdown. In our culture, that includes the promotion of alternative sexualities, this can result in some young people being confused about their sexuality. They may need help to understand and work through deeper-seated insecurities, issues of forgiveness, gender acceptance and self-acceptance before they can come to terms with their sexual identity.'* **Pastoral Guidelines – Homosexuality, Social Issues and Resources Panel**

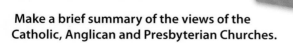

FOR YOUR FOLDER

Make a brief summary of the views of the Catholic, Anglican and Presbyterian Churches.

IN A GROUP

1. Explain why the issue of homosexuality causes controversy for the Christian Church.

2. Do you imagine that there will ever be a change of attitude regarding homosexuality among the leadership of these churches?

FURTHER THINKING

What Bible texts shape the Churches' views on homosexuality?

FURTHER THINKING

Divide into groups of four.

Choose one of the following topics to research. Find out what the different Christian denominations have to say about the issue.

Use the internet or interview your local priest or minister

Present your findings to the class.

Some examples to consider:

- The age of consent
- Alcohol and drug use
- Christian involvement in politics
- Same-sex marriage blessings
- Attitudes to war
- Responsibility towards the environment
- Treatment for infertility

CLASS DEBATE

"The teachings of the Bible do not change, so the attitude of the churches to moral issues should not change."

Do you agree or disagree? Give reasons for your answer.

FOR YOUR FOLDER

1. Describe the work of one organisation which helps bring together Christians from different traditions.

2. Why do many Christians think that it is important to understand the beliefs and values of traditions different from their own?

3. Do you think the Christian Church has the right to speak out about changing moral standards in our society? Give reasons for your answer, showing that you have considered more than one point of view.

Index

Abortion 120, 121
Advent 75–79, 84, 87
Ambo 68, 69
Angel 13–16, 18, 50
Anointing 33, 95, 98
Annunciation 13, 53
Ascension 13, 46, 76, 110
Ash Wednesday 84, 85, 87

Baptism 5, 12, 16, 17, 21, 70–74, 84, 92, 95–107
Bethlehem 6, 14, 15, 16, 79
Bible 5, 16, 47, 52, 53, 55
Bread 18, 36, 37, 52, 53, 55, 56, 59, 63, 68–70, 72, 74, 107–114

Charismatic 48
Charity 8, 28, 29, 82, 86, 87, 93, 118
Christmas 15, 16, 49, 75–84, 91, 92
Communion 37, 47, 56, 57, 59, 60, 61, 66, 70, 72, 73
Container Ministry 94
Corrymeela 115, 116
Covenant 24, 26, 36, 104, 106, 107
Cross 41, 54, 56, 61, 68, 70, 73, 74, 85, 87–89, 91, 96, 98–100, 103, 104, 111, 112, 115, 116
Crucifixion 34, 40–43, 89, 91, 108
Cruciform 66, 68, 70, 71

David 6, 12, 13, 14, 77
Death 5, 7, 8, 11–14, 16, 20, 21, 34, 36–45, 52, 56, 67, 87, 88, 91, 98, 100–102, 105–108, 110–114, 122
Debt 27
Devil 18, 19, 99
Disciple 12, 13, 17, 20–24, 30, 33–38, 42–45, 52, 88, 95, 100, 105, 107, 109, 112, 113

Easter 49, 70, 76, 84, 85, 87, 88, 89, 90, 91, 92, 96, 106
Elijah 17, 18, 20, 21, 41
Elizabeth 14
Embrace 118
Empire 7, 13, 39, 46
Eucharist 37, 50, 51, 55, 56, 63, 66, 68–70, 78, 95, 97, 98, 107, 108, 109, 114

Fasting 18, 24, 28, 75, 85–88
Festival 6, 36, 61, 75, 76, 78, 79, 80, 84, 85, 88, 90, 91, 93
Font 70, 71, 73, 74, 97, 99, 102–104
Forgiveness 26–28, 35, 36, 42, 50, 52, 55, 61, 85, 100, 109

Galilee 6–9, 11, 17, 35, 45
Gentile 9, 10, 11, 15, 23, 24, 33
Golgotha 40, 42
Good Friday 85, 87–91
Gospel 5, 8, 11–1, 16, 18, 20, 23, 30, 33, 34, 43, 45, 46, 52, 53, 55, 63, 64, 69, 71, 79, 81, 89, 92
Gothic 66, 67
Great Commission 45, 46, 95

Harvest 76, 93, 94
Hate 8, 25, 26
Heal 13, 23, 29, 33, 48, 51, 83, 94
High Priest 8, 10–12, 38, 39, 42
Holy of Holies 10, 41, 42, 68
Homosexuality 120, 123-125
Hypocrites 11, 24, 28, 31, 32

Incarnation 16, 77
Isaiah 12, 14, 17, 41, 77
Israel 5, 10–14, 19, 24, 31, 36, 37, 41, 47

Jerusalem 7, 7, 13, 16, 40, 68, 70, 87
John the Baptist 6, 14, 16, 17, 18, 20
Joseph 13–15, 54, 79, 88, 93
Judaism 8, 11, 20, 21
Judas 36, 38, 43
Judea 6, 7, 8, 11, 17, 35
Judgement 34, 36, 41

King 12–15, 17, 27, 34, 40, 41, 77
Kingdom of God (Kingdom of heaven) 16, 18, 23, 25, 33, 88, 100
King of the Jews 15, 40, 41

Last Supper 36, 37, 56, 88, 107, 109, 112, 113
Law 8, 9, 11, 14, 20–22, 24, 26, 31, 32, 34, 38, 39
Lectern 71, 72–74
Lectionary 57, 60
Lent 19, 76, 78, 84–87
Liturgy 47, 48, 55, 57, 58, 60, 68, 70, 71, 75, 77, 109
Lord's Prayer 47, 52, 54, 57, 60, 63, 100, 110
Love 18, 26, 27, 30, 32, 53, 56, 57, 58, 59, 61, 62, 78, 88, 93, 103, 104, 109, 110, 112, 120, 122

Magi 15, 16, 76, 79, 81, 84
Martin Luther King Jr 26
Mary 13–15, 33, 34, 43, 50, 53, 79, 97
Messiah 6,11, 12, 13, 15, 17–20, 34, 35, 38–41, 43, 76,77

Miracle 14, 18, 20, 21, 33, 83
Money (wealth) 8, 10, 22, 26, 28, 29, 34, 55, 58, 59, 61, 62, 81, 82, 86, 88, 109, 110
Moses 8, 12, 20, 21, 24, 31, 32, 69

New Covenant 24, 106, 107
Nightlight 118
Novenas 54

Oral Law 8
Ordinances (see Sacraments)
Outreach 117, 118

Palestine 5–9, 12, 33, 38, 40
Palm Sunday 40, 87, 89
Parable 24, 25, 27, 28, 29, 30
Parousia (see 'Second Coming')
Passion 89, 108
Passover 36, 37, 40, 107, 108
Pentecost 48, 92
Peter (Simon Peter) 12, 20, 21, 27, 28, 38, 43, 83
Pharisee 8, 11, 24, 25, 31, 32, 34, 38
Pilate 7, 39, 40
Prayer 9, 24, 25, 28, 31, 37, 47, 50–64, 78, 85, 87, 88, 89, 93, 94, 97, 99–114, 122
Preaching 17, 64, 92
Prophecy 12, 13, 14, 17, 38, 39, 48
Protestant 37, 50–52, 55, 63, 68, 87, 93, 95, 108, 115, 117
Psalm 17, 40, 41, 48, 61–64
Pulpit 62, 66, 69, 70, 71–74

Rabbi 22, 25
Red Nose Day 29
Resurrection 5, 11, 12, 13, 36, 43–45, 56, 67, 68, 70, 76, 88, 89, 91, 97, 100, 102, 105, 108, 110, 11, 112, 113
Revenge 26
River Jordan 6, 17
Roman 7, 8, 11, 12, 20, 25, 33, 38–43, 46, 91
Rosary 53

Sabbath 9
Sacraments (Ordinances) 70, 88, 95–103, 106, 108, 110, 113
Sacrifice 10, 13, 22,23, 36, 42, 55, 56, 68, 88, 107, 108, 109
Saint 50, 54, 55, 56, 75, 92, 93, 98
Salvation Army 82, 95
Samaria 6, 7, 35
Sanhedrin 8, 11, 13, 38–40
Saviour 11, 13, 15, 69, 96, 101, 104
Scribes 8, 11, 31, 34

Scripture 9, 14, 16, 18, 19, 21, 26, 31, 35, 40, 41, 53, 57, 59–61, 68, 71–74, 96, 101, 121, 124
Second Coming (parousia) 72, 111, 112, 114
Sermon 47, 61–65, 70–74
Sermon on the Mount 24, 26
Shepherds 15, 79
Son of David 13, 33
Son of God 12, 13, 21, 42, 69, 84
Son of Man 13, 17, 20, 21, 22, 39
Spirit 14, 17, 48, 61, 64, 79, 81, 92, 97, 99, 101, 103, 104, 106, 113
St Vincent De Paul 118, 119
Storehouse 118
Suffering servant 12, 41
Synagogue 9, 24, 32
Synoptic Gospels 5, 23

Tax 7, 8, 11, 24, 25
Temple 10, 16, 18, 25, 39, 40–42, 68
Temptation 5, 16, 18, 19, 38, 52
Ten Commandments 8, 24
Tomb 32, 42–44, 88, 91
Transfiguration 12, 20, 21, 38, 84
Transubstantiation 37, 69, 108, 109
Trócaire 86

Unclean 8, 11, 32
Universalism 33, 35

Vineyard 118

Wine 32, 36, 37, 55, 56, 59, 68–70, 72, 107–114
Women 10, 31, 33, 35, 43, 44, 47, 93, 101, 124

Zealots 7, 11, 40

Acknowledgements

Picture credits

iStockphoto: Cover, 5 (left), 6 (top left), 7 (right), 8 (top left, middle, bottom right), 12 (left), 13, 15 (left, top right), 17 (both), 18 (both), 20 (bottom left, top right), 21, 22, 27 (both), 29, 31 (bottom), 32, 34, 37 (both), 38, 39 (bottom right), 40 (top right), 41 (top), 42 (right), 44, 45, 48 (top), 50, 59 (left), 64, 75 (left), 77 (top right), 81, 84 (both), 85 (both), 88 (left, top right), 91 (top left), 92 (left), 95 (right),96, 98 (top right), 99, 108 (bottom), 116 (right), 117, 118 (top right), 121, 122, 123, 125

CrossTalk: 49 (top left), 54 (right), 56 (top), 68, 69 (all), 70 (both), 71 (all), 72 (all left), 73 (all), 74(all), 101, 112

Alex Eleon: 6 (bottom left)
Shutterstock: 7 (left)
Masqueraid: 9 (bottom)
Deror Avi: 10 (top)
Gugganij: 20 (Top left)
Michael Spence: 41 (bottom), 42 (left), 77 (bottom right)
Jamie Artt: 48 (bottom), 49 (top right)
Rob Elkin: 49 (middle right)
Norman Johnston: 49 (bottom left),58 (left), 60, 68, 72 (both right), 104
Anne Hughes: 54 (left), 79 (bottom left), 119 (left)
Allan Barton: 77 (left)

Ruth Laverty: 78 (top)
Wesley Fryer: 80 (bottom right)
Stephen Dwyer: 88 (bottom right)
Marcin Szala: 92 (right)
Maros Mraz: 93 (left)
Beth Peat: 93 (right)
Tim Dunwoody: 94
Tom Adrianenssen: 97
David Ball: 102
Corrymeela Community: 115
Mark Weir: 116 (left)
Juliana Gilbride: 119

Copyright information

The logos of Red Nose Day (page 29), the Salvation Army (page 82), Trócaire (page 86) the Corrymeela Community (page 115), Embrace NI (page 118) and SVP (page 118) appear by kind permission of these organisations.

The following images are licensed under the GNU Free Doumentation License. Permission is granted to copy, distribute and/or modify these documents under the terms of the GNU Free Documentation License, Version 2.1 or any later version published by the Free Software Foundation; with no Invariant Sections, no Front-Cover Texts and no Back-Cover Texts. A copy of the license can be viewed at http://www.fsf.org/licensing/licenses/fdl.html

Page 9 (bottom) retrieved from http://upload.wikimedia.org/wikipedia/commons/e/e0/Ruins_of_the_Ancient_Synagogue_at_Bar%27am.jpg

Page 20 (top left) retrieved from http://upload.wikimedia.org/wikipedia/commons/2/2e/Banias_Spring_Cliff_Pan%27s_Cave.JPG

Martin Luther King Jr. quotes on page 23 reprinted by arrangement with The Heirs to the Estate of Martin Luther King Jr., c/o Writers House as agent for the proprietor New York, NY. Copyright 1963 Dr. Martin Luther King Jr; copyright renewed 1986 Coretta Scott King

Copyright has been acknowledged to the best of our ability. If there are any inadvertent errors or omissions, we shall be happy to correct them in any future editions.